EBURY PRESS

THE LIVING ROAD

Ajit Harisinghani is a speech therapist by profession and a traveller by passion. He lives in Pune, with his wife and daughter. *The Living Road* is his second book.

T0001438

THE LIVING ROAD

A MOTORCYCLE
JOURNEY TO
BHUTAN

AJIT HARISINGHANI

EBURY
PRESS

An imprint of Penguin Random House

EBURY PRESS

USA | Canada | UK | Ireland | Australia
New Zealand | India | South Africa | China

Ebury Press is part of the Penguin Random House group of companies
whose addresses can be found at global.penguinrandomhouse.com

Published by Penguin Random House India Pvt. Ltd
4th Floor, Capital Tower 1, MG Road,
Gurugram 122 002, Haryana, India

Penguin
Random House
India

First published by Westland Ltd 2015
Published in Ebury Press by Penguin Random House India 2022

Copyright © Ajit Harisinghani 2015

ISBN 9780143458555

Typeset in Dante MT by SÜRYA, New Delhi
Printed at Replika Press Pvt. Ltd, India

www.penguin.co.in

For Meena and Juhi

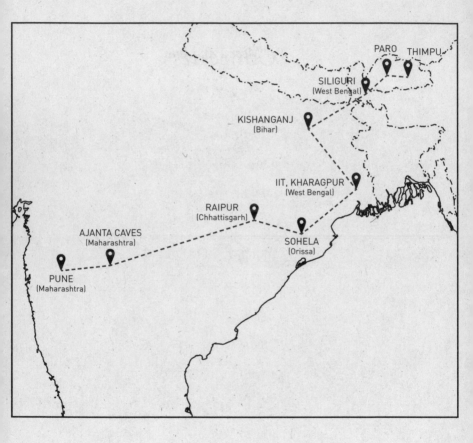

Contents

Prologue   1

Bhutan on My Mind   9

First Day on the Road   15

The Singing Goat of Meherabad   21

Celebrating Buddha in the Ajanta Caves   27

Akola Anyone?   31

Nagzira   38

Dhaba Guru   52

Time For a Joke?   58

IIT Kharagpur   77

Strikes and Broken Bridges   85

Kishanganj   94

Elephant, Ahoy!   102

Entering Bhutan   109

A Paradise Called Gedu   120

Thimpu   129

Paro   139

I'm on Bhutan TV   147

Back to India   155

Epilogue   162

Acknowledgements   165

Prologue

SUNDAY IS JUST about winding up when my cell phone buzzes. I wonder who is calling so late. It's almost midnight. I press the answer button and say, 'Hello.'

'Hello, sir. I am Rahul Bhatia calling from Nagpur. Remember me?'

Food and drink have diverted blood to my stomach and my brain is not at its alert best. I have no idea who the caller is. I'm ready to sleep and am in a half-daze already. Besides, Rahul is a common enough name.

What he says next jerks me sober.

'Sir, I am committing suicide.'

'What…? Who…? Where are you?' I finally ask.

'In Ambajari park, sir, cyanide in my hand.'

I wonder if this is a hoax but the desperate voice sounds genuine enough.

'Sir, I just wanted to thank you for all you did, but I

can't take it anymore. I had improved but my stammering has returned. I want to die. I'm useless. I can't even speak properly.' He is sobbing and I'm still trying to recollect who he is. Obviously one of my old clients but I can't remember his face.

'And, you know... my father...today he got angry when I stammered while attending to a customer. I am worthless...how will I run the business? I can't even speak properly. What's the use of living like this?'

As I listen, I try to find a way to deflect his suicidal thoughts.

'Rahul,' I say, 'thank you very much for calling me. Really, I'm quite flattered that you thought of talking to me at this momentous time in your life—the time of your death! I can't wish you all the best, or even a *bon voyage* because I don't know what happens to souls who have committed suicide. Do they regret it? Want to reverse it, but can't? I guess we'll never know.'

I ask him if he could defer committing suicide for a week. He could come say his goodbyes in person. A long silence follows and then he says, 'Yes, but only if you promise not to try and stop me.'

I tell him that, in fact, I will help him commit suicide, but a week from today.

'In any case,' I point out, 'no one is really waiting for you "up there". In fact they're not expecting your arrival for six and a half more decades!'

The lightness and irreverent humour in my voice must

have surprised him. Maybe he expected me to panic and try to stop him from killing himself. Maybe that is the reason he had called me in the first place—to get some dramatic attention? After all, he was ending his life and wanted at least one onlooker. Whatever he felt, my response seems to have deflated the pressurized balloon of his mind, which I pictured was slowly coming back to earth.

He sounds a bit calmer now, says okay, he will throw away the cyanide. I ask him how he'd got hold of it in the first place and he says, 'Don't you remember? My father has a sports trophy workshop where cyanide is used to etch metal?' I tell him to be careful where he disposes it. A non-suicidal animal in the park might ingest it by mistake and die. He actually laughs at that one and agrees to come to Pune for a personal goodbye. Is that relief I hear in his voice, or am I just imagining it? After all, it's a seven-day respite from self-execution. One more week to live!

I wish him a good night and get ready to slide into slumber land myself. It's been a long day. But Rahul with his pinch of cyanide keeps intruding into my thoughts, not letting me sleep. I switch on my laptop and open up the case-records' files. There he is.

Rahul Bhatia.

Age: 22.

Resident of Nagpur.

Only son of a businessman.

I remember him now—a personable young man with

a very slight stammering problem. He'd attended three sessions during which he'd told me he was constantly afraid of being laughed at because of the way he talked. His father was another source of stress, pushing him into the family business.

As I read through his case history, I wonder if my gamble has worked. Could he have been too far gone and dead already? Cyanide is known to be quick. I imagine him lying frothing at the mouth in a dark Nagpur park. Unsettling thoughts...can't seem to switch them off. Having long passed the age for my mother to sing me to sleep with a lullaby, I pick up the remote to switch the TV on, hoping to catch a boring programme. That generally does the trick. Not this time though. Channel-surfing, I pause on a popular news network to admire a charming, sari-clad woman with a diamond-stud in her nose and Madhubala-lips. The camera then moves to focus on the person she is conversing with. A handsome, regal, middle-aged man, dressed in an unusual, maroon, knee length, checked-tweed garment is talking in the calm and unhurried manner of someone used to being listened to. Interested, I put the remote down and watch. The lady is addressing him as Your Majesty. Then a bottom caption confirms that it is indeed royalty I am listening to. His Royal Highness Jigme Singye Wangchuk, King of Bhutan!

He is saying that not GNP (Gross National Product) but GNH (Gross National Happiness) should be the true measure of a society's progress. While economic prosperity is important, richer countries are not necessarily happier ones. Rarely have I heard a ruler talk with such gut sanity. When the King's speech is over, I wave my wand, the TV shuts off.

Maybe Rahul should go to Bhutan to find happiness? Maybe we should all go to Bhutan. Maybe I should go to Bhutan. I go to sleep hugging the nascent plan to take off on my motorbike and go find this Promised Land and bring back a chunk of happiness to share with the Rahuls of this world. My dream that night is an audio-visual fantasy where I am riding an undulating road coursing through the green, green hills of Bhutan where the branches of the road-side trees are bent; loaded as they are with an iridescent fruit which, legend guarantees, grants everlasting happiness to everyone who eats it.

A day later, Rahul arrives on the early morning bus and comes straight to the clinic looking disoriented, his face frozen in stress. Well, what did I expect? Here was someone who only 48 hours ago had been ready to kill himself.

'Sir, I am scared... just scared... so scared to die... You saved me that night or I would have done it.' I gesture him to sit and pour him a glass of water which he gulps down too hastily, gags and then spends the next minute coughing. Once he's settled, I ask him what had triggered Sunday night's drama. That starts him off on a litany against his father who has been forcing him to join the family business which he has no interest in. He actually wants to work with cars but his father won't hear of it.

'What! You want to be a mechanic?'

Over and over again during the next two days' sessions, he dives into the sea of his misery to come up with nuggets of problems and 'FATHER' is written on most of them. The problems keep coming. No one cares for him. He is so lonely. I listen and listen till I near the limits of my own tolerance. The list of his complaints seems long indeed. I advise him to write out all his problems, and bring me this complete list the next day. I caution him not to miss mentioning any. Even the smaller problems should be on tomorrow's list.

The following day, his list is ready—all four tightly packed A4-sized pages of it. I take the list from him and spend the next ten minutes reading it out aloud. I then signal him to follow me out to the open porch where I take out my cigarette lighter and click the paper afire.

'There...no more problems! You are now free.'

I affect a calm expression on my face but inside I am not sure which way this would go. Will it shake him off his track of self-pity or, will he get angry and hysterical?

He doesn't say anything for a minute but his sly, knowing look tells me he is sticking to his stand.

'Are you trying to stop me? I'm here just to wish you goodbye. I am planning to commit suicide, remember? And you said you would help me do it.'

Yesterday he was scared of death. Today, he is afraid to live!

When I put my arm around his shoulder I feel him flinch. Tactile defensiveness—a classic feature of the un-loved.

'Sure, commit suicide. I've promised to aid and abet it,' I tell him. 'But let us first decide who or what are we trying to kill here. Who is our intended victim?' Rahul says he doesn't understand what I am trying to say. Isn't it clear that he, Rahul, was the victim?

'It is your mind that you need to murder, not your body,' is my reply. 'You don't hate your legs do you? Or your eyes? What about your arms? Your liver? Your heart, your lungs? You have no real grouse against them, do you? So why kill these innocent organs? Commit suicide of your mind. That's where your problems are lodged. If you hate being Rahul, become someone else. Drop your father. You're sinking under his weight. Become your own boss. Rebel! Every generation must rebel. That is how evolution takes place. Imagine where we'd all be if the caveman's son had listened to his father and not ventured out? Rebel... Drop your past!'

For the two weeks he stayed in Pune, Rahul changed his name to Vikrant. He, the son of a rich businessman, took up a job as a waiter at the Darshan Hotel on Karve Road. The owner, an old friend, on my request, had consented to give him a job. One of his regular waiters was on leave and he was looking for help anyway.

At the hotel, Rahul was on his feet all day long. He

lived a lifestyle totally alien to him. For two weeks, he slept near the hotel in a shack with some other (genuine) waiters. He had no time for his speech sessions with me. His job allowed him no rest. Only work and sleep. No time to feed his self-pity.

The following week, I had to leave town. By the time I returned, Rahul was gone. My hotel owner friend said he had left suddenly. Not even taken the salary due to him. I called his mobile number and was told in three languages that it did not exist.

I hoped the same did not apply to its owner.

Bhutan on My Mind

IT'S BEEN THREE years since I physically came back from the Ladakh ride. Mentally, I'm often still there. Ladakh is hard to shake off. You wouldn't know it if you saw me sitting in my chair, eyes closed, apparently playing footsie with myself, but chances are you're only seeing the shell. I'm not inside. Either I'm away re-trudging the 10,000 feet high undulating desert road of the Morey plains or, I could be on Khardung La, being re-chilled to the bone by my glacier-soaked shoes and socks. It might be a hot summer's day in Pune, 38 degrees Celsius outside, but not for me. I am sitting on that large black rock overlooking Suraj Tal, cleaning snow from the sole. Mental teleportation? One way to beat the heat! Works for a while but enjoyable as nostalgia is, I'm satiated with three years of wading through it.

An urge to get back on the road is beginning to grip me

again. Probably what migratory birds feel in their insides a few days before they finally embark on those long, long flights. Birds have an advantage in that they seem to know exactly where to go and when. I don't. Various destinations are vying for first place in my mind. Jaisalmer almost wins, but the image of a lone rider on an arrow-straight road, cutting through a stark brown desert gets pushed into second place by the memory of His Majesty King Wangchuk of Bhutan. His thoughts on GNH get me thinking of Bhutan. Maybe postpone Jaisalmer to next year? That's not really a long ride, just 1500 kilometres. I want to go at least double that distance… must allow time for the road to seep into the bones… Bhutan must be fascinating—the Land of the Thunder Dragon. Could it really be a country of happy people? My Road Atlas says Pune to Thimpu is 3000 kms. Perfect!

I've decided on a mid-October departure. The schools will not have closed yet and my case load will not be heavy. It is during the holidays that the clinic turns busy. Octobers are a good month to be riding a motorcycle across India for reasons of weather too. The blistering heat of the summer has been subdued by three months of rain. It's still hot but not uncomfortably so. Trees have fresh foliage so roads have grottos of shade, ideal for those short halts. The rivers and lakes are full. Harvests have been reaped and festivity and abundance is in the air. The major festivals of Durga Puja and Dussera are just around the corner and Diwali is coming up. October signals the beginning of the happy season in India.

'But, Baba...Why on a motorcycle? It's so unsafe. What are you trying to prove? Why can't you just take the train?' asks Juhi who has just stepped into her teens and is convinced I am a bit crazy. She knows that to get to Bhutan, I'll have to ride through some 'rough' areas. She warns me that I could get robbed, kidnapped or even killed. She reads out reports of such news hoping to scare me into abandoning what she thinks is a suicidal venture. She doesn't say it but I know she also thinks I'm too old for such a physically demanding task.

'At least go with a group,' she says attempting a semi-compromise. I tell her that no one is really alone on the roads of India—at least on the ones I'll be riding on this time. Experience has taught me, help is always available on an Indian highway, sometimes even when you don't want it.

Besides, a group-ride can easily turn into a picnic.

In retrospect, I realize that I never did ask myself whether or not I'd actually be able to do it. I don't know what my answer would have been. Ask no questions and be told no lies!

I've allowed myself a month off from needing to don my speech therapist's garb. Twenty days on the road with an extra ten for any contingencies encountered. Anything can happen on an Indian road and it'd be a pity if nothing does. That's the reason I'm on this ride in the first place—for the insecurity of it. If I wanted only to be safe, I'd have taken Juhi's advice and gone on a streamlined group tour organized by a travel company that prides itself for its reliability and predictability. Some agencies even take cooks along to provide the same food one would eat at home.

To those who consider security to be paramount, a solo motorcycle ride through India is strongly *not* recommended. Don't get me wrong. I'm no Rambo and am quite keen on self-preservation. I'll take all precautions against bike, body, or even mind failure and still be ready to handle the unforeseen when it happens. It is a kind of self-diagnostic check-up for my fifty-seven-year-old body. It is also the time alone that I seek, away from the routine activities of daily living. Away from solving (speech) problems of others and trying to deal with a few of my own! A solo bike ride through central and eastern India holds that promise of self-therapy.

Any kind of adventurous travel is a quest for the unexpected. In a manner of speaking, I am looking for trouble. An uneventful trip where nothing went wrong and nothing unexpected happened is no fun. So I'm hoping for many unusual things to happen to me. My professional work puts me in the role of the counsellor and I find myself advising other people on how they could best handle the issues that they are facing. I want to see how I deal with unexpected issues. Put my money where my mouth is.

Down in the garage the motorcycle stands primed for departure. It's a 1995 Royal Enfield 350 cc Standard, and we are old travelling buddies; me and my steed of steel. I know it's all in my mind but I do feel a kinship with this hunk of metal. It is in as perfect a shape as a middle-aged machine can hope to be. Leaks a drop or two of oil—as if there's a prostrate problem, (one of us had to have it!).

It has received some serious attention at the workshop. The piston now has new rings that achieve tighter closure with the cylinder. Everything that needs to has been replaced, lubricated, tightened or adjusted. It's performed nicely in the last week that I've been test-riding it. The slight oil-leak persists in spite of new gaskets and fresh sealant. My mechanic, not normally known for his sense of humour, says, 'It's NOT leaking. It's just marking its territory. Like a tiger!'

In every other way the bike is now 'better than new', which is more than what I can say for myself.

Three years back, before embarking on the Ladakh ride, I had cycled and exercised and got myself physically fit. This time I'm going on an as-is-where-is basis. These last few years, I've not being paying much attention to my body. It's been a fairly well behaved bag of organs and after all, what use are organs if they aren't organized? On my part, I've been pampering them with all sorts of tasty solid, liquid and aromatic rewards.

I suspect the Ladakh ride has turned me cocky. For one, I expect this ride to Bhutan to be a much easier journey than the one into the high Himalayas. Repeated visits to Google Earth have assured me that this time there will be no rugged, remote, ice-laden terrain to cross. No need to carry high-altitude gear. The highest point I'll touch will be Thimpu—no more than 3000 metres above sea level. Also, the roads I'll take are mainly national highways. Hotels, *dhabas*, service stations aplenty! I'm not taking the heavy foot-pump, just an extra tube. I prefer to replace the tube rather than repair the puncture. The few spares I'm carrying don't take up much space. Just cables, a plug and a set of electronic points, a pair of fuses. And of course a 1-litre can of engine oil for my territory-marking tiger.

I've planned to make this a comfortable trip and apart from packing some high nutrition foods and electrolytes, I've also included an electric tea maker for those early mornings when the cook is an hour away from waking up.

My army pal has arranged for my accommodation in three Officers' Messes in Bhutan and another friend, a road contractor, has used his political contacts to book me in the Circuit House in Akola and the MLA Hostel in Nagpur. I assuage any feelings of guilt for this personal use of government accommodation by telling myself that it is my tax money that's paying for it. To make it even easier on myself, I've broken up the 3000 kilometre route into shorter daily rides and resolved to go slower—take the element of 'hurry' out of my calculations. I've no records to break.

In any case, riding solo, one is sure of coming first.

First Day on the Road

LAST NIGHT I finished packing. The saddle bags are loaded and strapped across the rear seat. The tank is full. It's the hour before departure and I'm thinking detail. Have I taken everything I might possibly need? Yes, I have.

The old canvass saddle-bags, reinforced with patches of leather, hang over the rear seat, held firm by two heavy-rubber straps. This time I'm paying particular attention to food and have packed in a box of high-protein *laddoos*, a packet each of almonds and cashew nuts and a quarter-litre bottle of lemon concentrate which when mixed with water, a pinch of salt and a spoon of powdered sugar makes a wonderful restorative of the body's electrolytes.

All bags packed, breakfast eaten, coffee drunk, good-byes said, helmet on, I get astride the motorcycle and kick-start the anxious engine which immediately begins to purr its favourite beat...dugh...dugh...dugh...dugh. The familiar roads of my city are now taking me out of it.

My destination for the day is Meherabad which is near Ahmednagar and only about 130 kms away. By 10, I am out of the crowded Monday morning Pune and onto the wide Ahmednagar Highway which now stretches straight ahead, cutting through a dry and rocky brown landscape.

I'm keeping my mind blank and not letting any internal thought-chatter intrude. I don't want to think about anything. I want to just feel the world and my place in it.

The sound of the engine and the beat of my heart have synchronized and become one. The wheels are my legs or should it be said the other way around—my legs have become wheels and acquired the speed and grace of a galloping gazelle? The breeze fills up the inside of my shirt and makes it flutter; tickling my chest as if trying to make me laugh. Mirages form ahead of me and miraculously disappear as I come upon them.

The dirty woollen rag in the middle of the road is actually a dead cat, run over by I don't know how many vehicles. I wonder how it got itself knocked off. The wide road offers a clear view in either direction. But it must all look different to a cat.

I stop for tea in Shirur and carry the taste of the thick oversweet brew on my tongue as I manoeuvre through a crowded market with shops on both sides of the road. They are all well stocked—their wares overflowing onto the pavement. Some shops are selling steel utensils while others are full of plastic buckets and chairs of various colours. For a while, I'm crawling behind a horse cart loaded with bars of construction steel. They stick out like spears behind the cart. A bright red cloth is tied to one of the bars and warns me to be watchful as I overtake the clip-clopping horse. The brown and white animal is effortlessly pulling what must be at least 500 kilos not counting the emaciated, bone-thin driver who is sitting astride over a portion of the load and has steel bars sticking out between his thighs. Soon I leave this scene, this town and the road opens up again.

It's been an uneventful ride so far. A broad highway can get monotonous after a while. Fast moving trucks and buses whizzing past mean that I have to maintain a heightened degree of awareness. I am passing through a mainly industrialized belt. The highway is lined on both sides by large factories manufacturing familiar branded consumer goods. Commerce rules the ambience here. Everyone seems intent on being a success. Ambition is in the air. Whoa! Good luck to them... Me? I'm retired from any work... for the whole of this month.

It is past noon as I come up to the outskirts of Ahmednagar and turn off the highway, at Kinetic Chowk for the last 10 kilometres to Meherabad, via Arangaon. This road suddenly becomes narrow and crowded and I weave my way through an ever-changing collage of stopped trucks, slow moving bullock carts, speeding buses and sprinting dogs; in other words, a typical road in India.

In the US, the well maintained tarmacs stretch straight and sure over vast distances with not a pothole or cow in sight. They lull and dull the mind into complacency with their lack of surprise. Not so here. Riding on the roads of India requires complete alertness. There are a zillion things to watch out for. Overloaded trucks and buses, fast cars and slow bullock carts are only a few on a long list of hazards. There are the pedestrians of course, but you must also try and avoid crashing into the vast variety of non-zoo animals that seem to have made the highway their home. Sitting in the middle of the road, totally unconcerned with all the traffic whizzing inches from their nose, are plenty of complacent cows. Don't they have a survival instinct or something? Or have centuries of deification by the masses embedded their DNA with an assurance-gene that guarantees complete immunity from harm? Then there are dogs, cats, chickens, ducks, pigs, goats, sheep, donkeys, horses, camels and yes, even the occasional elephant ambling along slowly, caring not a hoot for traffic rules, frisking its tail between its huge buttocks in a gesture that could very well be daring the honking truckers to kiss its arse!

While American roads offer predictable safety, Indian

roads compensate by providing unending entertainment, and even some opportunities for self growth. An Indian road is a stage where Life seems to be unabashedly living itself out.

Just after you saw the three raggedy children squatting and relieving themselves by the side of the road (chit chatting with each other even as their digestive systems were evacuating), you see a bejewelled but bewildered young groom on a huge white horse which is taking him to his bride-to-be. Everyone else around him looks deliriously happy, dancing and singing but he doesn't look at ease. It could be the horse that's scaring him or is it the prospect of marrying a girl he has probably not even seen yet that's making him tense?

Few hours later you slow down to crawl behind a funeral procession. Four pall bearers effortlessly carrying the white-cloth draped, marigold covered corpse bouncing on a flimsy bamboo stretcher, with about twenty mourners in tow. Everyone is chanting *Ram Naam Satya Hai* (Ram's Name is Truth). No one, not even the pall bearers, look particularly sad. Life goes on with its nitty-gritty details right along this one that has just ended.

Finally, a closed railway crossing is all that separates me from my destination for the day. I join the crowd of waiting vehicles, switch off the engine, take the helmet off and wait for the train to pass. These last few hours, aided by breeze on the moving bike, I've been unaware of the rising temperature but now that I've stopped, the hot dry air makes its presence felt, first on my sparse scalp and then on my face. Presently the earth trembles as two sturdy looking engines pull a freight train past us. I am automatically impelled to count the rakes—sixty-eight, sixty-nine, seventy—and then the final guard's cabin with its lone black-coated guard holding green and red flags. The fading rickety-rick of the train is now masked out by a cacophony of car and scooter horns, everyone impatiently urging the gate keeper to be quick. A thin, middle-aged man emerges from a tiny room and makes the universal gesture for 'wait, wait', with his hand, then unhurriedly walks up to the gate, unlocks and opens it, stepping quickly aside to avoid the onrush of assorted traffic. I too ride across the tracks and enter Meherabad where I am meeting my friend Krishna.

The Singing Goat of Meherabad

KRISHNA IS A singer and a physicist, and although we met only a few months back, we have become friends. He has moved back to India after many years of living in the US where he got his PhD in laser physics and was then teaching in upstate New York. Last year, he chucked his American life and returned to India to pursue his passion which was the study of classical vocal music. Krishna holds unique views on just about everything. That turns every meeting with him into a debate of ideas. I'm looking forward to meeting him here in Meherabad where he's taken up temporary abode in the home of his American friend.

I have the directions to his house. Turn right along the rail track, pass a house with a wooden gate and barking dogs, turn left on an unpaved road, ride up a kilometre and look for a house of stone with a red tiled roof. One can hardly go wrong with such detailed instructions especially when there are no other roads branching out to confuse you. I ride up to the gate, stop and rev the engine. The loud sound gets the desired result. Krishna comes out of the house and walks towards me with a goat in tow.

Krishna looks like a yogi. Dense dark hair and beard frame a fair, well chiselled face. A wiry athletic physique stands testimony to the fact that he's a yoga fanatic. If you didn't know he was fifty-two, you'd say he was around thirty-two years old. Today he is bare-chested, bare-foot and wearing a barely white half dhoti which the goat seems intent to snatch. Krishna untangles goat-teeth from textile, shoos the animal away, looks at me and laughs. Readjusting his disturbed garment, he directs me to park in the open garage next to the main house. I put the bike up on its stand, unstrap the saddle bags and follow Krishna across a central courtyard to enter a small room which he tells me is John's office. It has a bed and the walls are crowded with books, most of them thick hardbound serious-looking tomes with titles that have words like Anthology, Consciousness, and such. John is American and the owner of the house. A Meher Baba follower, currently in Texas, he's letting Krishna use the lower section while he is away.

'Come, come. I've made *khichdi*,' Krishna says pointing to the pressure cooker whistling on the stove. The goat has followed us in and stands next to Krishna with its short tail wagging. I catch myself wishing the goat was in the cooker but curb that thought half-way. This is vegetarian land and I must not think of mutton *biryanis*, not with Yogiraj Krishna around!

'What's with the goat?' I ask anyway.

'Oh...Gori? I've got her on loan...for the milk...very nice, loving animal.'

'Is that why she was trying to undress you?' I ask and make him break into peals of laughter. I admire the ease and the free abandon of his laugh. It is as if he's living in a funnier world. I am soon to discover that the goat is kind of special too. And it's not my taste-buds that are talking here.

'You want to see something?' asks Krishna and bends down to tickle the animal's throat. It seems to be a trigger because suddenly Gori, the goat, breaks out into a loud bleat! Then a strange thing happens. The bleat steadies and sweetens. All goats I've heard so far have bleats that are hoarse and brief and, if you ever think about it, not really that pleasant. This goat was actually singing! I was hearing a sonorous Maaaaaaaaa Maaaaaaaaa Maaaaaaaaaaaaaaaaaa; not unlike the preliminary *alap* to a classical *raga*. Or was it a song celebrating mother's day in goat-land?

'I'm teaching her to maintain a stable *swar* (pitch). I have to squeeze a part of her voice box but she's learning to keep it steady on her own. Now watch this...' and he changes his grip on the goat's throat. The animal, as if suddenly reminded of paternal obligations, now breaks into a father's day song. Bbaaa...Bbaaaaaaaaaa...Baba. I listen, fascinated for a while.

'Enough. Now let's eat,' Krishna says and removes his hand from the goat's throat. The drone stops as if a switch has been flicked off. He leads her away, returns and gets the cooker off the stove.

The *khichdi* is delicious and easy on the stomach and suddenly I'm glad it is not mutton *biryani*. We all know the story where a young Gandhi ate goat meat for the first time and heard the animal bleating in his stomach for the next few days. That's when he had finally resolved to become vegetarian. I'm left wondering about the next time I eat mutton *biryani*. Will a goat start crooning inside me too? And if it does, will it croon in tune? Like Gori?

Meherabad is mainly a community of Parsis and Americans who call themselves 'Meher Baba Lovers'. From what I've heard from Krishna, I know that Meher Baba was an enlightened man who preached universal love and compassion. He passed away (or 'left his body' as his disciples are prone to say) in 1952. His followers have established Meherabad, a spread of around 100 acres of what was mainly arid land before they beautified it with trees and scattered lovely houses around the campus.

Seven pm is when everyone gets together at the Baba's *Samadhi*. It is a temple-like structure with an open courtyard which has a sitting level parapet around it. By the time Krishna and I arrive, a crowd of women, men and children have already gathered and everyone seems to be in a peppy, joyous mood. There is a peaceful, positive, loving energy in the air. A tall, well built man comes to greet Krishna and I meet Ben, a sixty-five-year-old New Yorker who supervises the running of the community kitchen. Ben is a retired Wall Street banker and now spends his time 'At Baba's feet' as he puts it. We sit together to hear the prayer which has just begun. Everyone around is singing it. When it is over, a young, jeans and T-shirt clad blonde puts a guitar in Krishna's hands. He sits on a stone parapet and begins to strum a Dylan song.

'Hey Mr Tambourine Man... Sing a Song for me... I'm not sleepy and there ain't no place I'm going to...'' When he finishes, the guitar-giving blonde sings a Joan Baez number. When that's over, everyone begins to disperse. Soon the venue is empty of people. We too walk back on the now darkened road that leads to John's house.

The next day dawn is predictably bright. Breakfast is yogi food. A white gruel of something which Krishna says is very healthy for us. He then suggests a change of itinerary. Instead of taking the highway to Nagpur, why don't I go via Ajanta? That will mean an additional 200 kilometres and an extra day but I really have no deadlines to meet. These ancient caves, said to be carved out in the mountains 2500 years ago by Buddhist monks, are a world heritage site, attracting people from all over the globe. Not to be missed. Krishna says he can ride with me to Ajanta and return home by bus the next day. I like the idea and open up my road atlas which shows me the route to the Ajanta caves via Aurangabad which will be a six-hour ride with halts.

I lug my saddle bags out to the bike and see that Gori is sitting perched up on the seat. Never seen such an agile goat! She sees me coming and jumps off the bike. I wipe off the few drops of milk that seem to have dripped from her udders onto the seat. I upload the saddle bags and shift my food-store onto the extended rear carrier. Now there's room for a pillion. When Krishna comes out with a backpack, the goat immediately gets up and walks towards him. 'She doesn't want me to leave,' he says as he drops his backpack, takes hold of one of her ears and gently leads her to the garage and ties her to a pole. He says he's phoned the owner who will come and take her away.

Krishna hops on behind me and as we make our way towards the gate, the goat begins to bleat a mournful 'bai...bai...bai' which soon gets masked by the more dominant sound of the motorcycle's revving engine.

Celebrating Buddha in the
Ajanta Caves

KRISHNA DOESN'T HAVE a helmet; he's covered his head-face-neck with a long black scarf leaving only slits for eyes. The bike feels heavier and less manoeuvrable with a pillion rider and compels me to go slow on the pot-holed and narrow road. Then it joins up with the highway and riding becomes easier all the way to Aurangabad.

The Ajanta Caves are located 100 kms northwest of Aurangabad. Billboards advertising the luxury, convenience or affordability of various hotels begin to vie for attention as we approach our destination.

The caves are quite a distance away from the area where the hotels are and it is too late to go there today. Looking for a suitable hotel, we chance upon a Maharashtra State police guest house. It is Krishna who spots it and yells for me to turn around and park next to the square two-storey building which has officious looking police vehicles parked around the open ground in front of it. Krishna says he can probably get us a room here. He has a cousin who is a big-shot in the Mumbai police and maybe our lodging could be arranged through his good offices. He says he has done this before. We walk up to the uniformed man sitting behind a receptionist's desk and Krishna mentions his cousin's name. A phone call is made and soon the required instructions are issued. We are allotted a large ground floor room with a balcony and promised dinner at 8 o'clock. Krishna's police officer cousin calls to check if everything is okay and I'm thinking, 'Nice cousin!'

The next morning, I decide to leave the bike parked safe within the guest house compound. The caves can be easily reached in an auto and soon, Krishna and I find ourselves trudging up the incline towards the first of the many caves which line the hillside. There are people everywhere. Groups of Indian and foreign tourists are gathered around guides who are revealing historic facts in the manner that only tourists guides do. Some of them are weathered veterans who look almost as old as the caves they are talking about. Over and over again for decades, they have repeated the story of these 2500-year-old caves, accidently discovered in 1819 by an Englishman while hunting chital in the then dense forests around these hills. Buddhist monks must have produced these magnificent stone sculptures and paintings after decades of labour and then, for some reason, abandoned their creation to the jungle where these had lain hidden for centuries.

At the base of the caves is a spread out landscaped park with a broad concrete road where a number of tourist buses are parked. A stone stairway leads up to the caves which stand with their open entrances facing the valley that dips below. Many are huge chambers with intricate figures carved into the walls, all narrating their own stories. The first few caves are crowded so we walk ahead and come to one with no one around. We enter and are momentarily blinded by the dark interior which gradually reveals a large hall leading to a smaller room. A ten-foot-high stone image of the seated Buddha occupies the inner space almost entirely. Two candles on the side walls cast wispy dancing shadows on all available surfaces, making the still Buddha appear to be shifting position. There is timelessness in the still air. Neither Krishna nor I can say a word. Silence rules. I move my eyes around the cave and travel back to the time when it was being carved. I imagine the stone-cutters conversing with each other (in Pali?) and now I can almost hear the clinks of their chisels as they chip away at the black rock. I can smell smoke in the unventilated room from wood burning torches. Must have been suffocating! Expert sculptors, balanced on ladders, are carving out intricate stories on every inch of the walls and the thirty-foot-high ceiling with basic tools. It must have taken years to complete. What drove them to work so hard for so long in such wilderness? Faith?

Suddenly Krishna starts singing.

Aaa Chalke Tujhe,
Main Leke Chaloo, Ik Aise Gagan ke Taley,
Jahan Gam Bhi Na Ho, Aasoo Bhi Na Ho,
Bas Pyaar hi Pyaar Pale.
Ik Aise Gagan ke Tale.
(Come let me take you,
To such a place under the sky,
Where there is no sadness, nor tears, just love,
Only love resides.
To such a place under the sky let me take you…)

His voice resonates in the confines of the cave. Natural acoustics, I suppose. Krishna finishes his song and as we turn around to leave, we find we've not been alone after all. A group of elderly German tourists and their old guide have been standing in a dark corner listening to the impromptu song. They smile and shake hands with us as we walk out. 'Wasn't that wonderful?' says the guide to his clients, as if he had arranged it all.

Trudging further up the rocky incline, we visit a few more of the thirty caves and then walk back to base where a rickshaw brings us back to the police guest house and my waiting motorcycle.

It is past noon as we ride to a dusty road crossing from where Krishna can get a bus back to Meherabad and I can get on the road to Akola.

Akola Anyone?

I GET BACK on the bike and point it towards Akola. The state highway I'm on, is coursing through an arid brown terrain punctuated by periodic habitations. I stop at a sugar cane juice stall which offers welcome shade from the hot ride. It has an old fashioned wooden crusher powered by a huge old bull which must have spent most of its adult life going around in circles. I plonk into a plastic chair and ask for their largest. The juice is served in a large brass glass and is frothing at the top like beer. I ask for ice but am told it's not available. No electricity here.

State Highway 24 takes me past Buldana, joins up with NH6 at Khamgaon from where it is 50 kilometres to my day's destination.

By dusk, I am in Akola which at first glance appears a haphazard kind of place. Nondescript buildings crowd both sides of the road and the sky space is dense with huge hoardings of photo-shopped politicians, who seem to be looking down on the general public with expressions of cultivated benevolence. Elections must be around the corner. There is an aggressive macho energy around the crowded main street I find myself on. Tired after a long day in saddle, I am anxious to end the day's ride and relax on an unmoving, non-vibrating chair.

Asking for directions, I finally locate and enter the grounds of the Circuit House. The spacious garden which surrounds the central building has many large trees with a lawn in front of the reception patio. At the desk, the clerk tells me he's sorry but he's received no instructions from anyone and as such, no room has been booked for me. I ask him for his mobile number, then call Suresh, my friend with 'contacts', and explain the situation. He says it's no problem and advises me to wait. I walk around the darkened garden for a while before the receptionist summons me to say that I've been allotted a suite on the first floor. Relieved, I trudge upstairs behind the bell boy who is helping with the luggage. Upstairs, a coir carpeted corridor leads to two adjacent suites one of which is to be mine for tonight. It is a three-room affair with everything a senior government official or visiting politician might possibly need for a comfortable stay. The bed is king sized as is the TV and the refrigerator. It feels great to be enjoying this luxury at government expense—the sweet taste of forbidden fruit.

A peg of Old Monk, a light dinner and a cigarette later,

I lie down on the bed and close my eyes, filtering out the barrage of thoughts till only one is left—Krishna's cave song accompanied by the image of an aged bull on an endless journey...going round and round and round...

Even though I wake up at six, I am in no particular hurry to leave this nice suite. My destination today is Nagpur, only about 250 kms away which, even at a leisurely pace should not take me more than eight hours. Actually, it takes six as the surface and the width of NH6 are good enough to allow me to go at a steady 80 kmph. That also means that the ride demands total focus. This is a major highway with fast moving, loaded trucks, buses, and SUVs which are the most aggressive. I keep to the slower lane on the extreme left of the highway and my steady pace brings me into the big city without incident.

Summer temperatures in Nagpur are known to touch 50 degrees but this is the middle of October and the city is at a pleasant 32°C, as I ask my way to the MLA Hostel where the ever helpful Suresh has managed to book me a room courtesy another 'contact'. Unsurprisingly, it is a pleasant building standing amidst a garden located in the quieter and cleaner part of the city. This time there is no glitch at the reception desk. Suite no. 2 on the ground floor has been reserved in my name for two days. Saying a silent thank you to Suresh and a loud one to the man at the desk, I take the proffered key and walk to Suite 2. When I unlock the door I find that it is really one large room, partitioned into two by a portable plywood screen with the bedroom on the other side. A far cry from the luxury of the Circuit House in Akola, but I'm not complaining. All I really need is a bed for a night. Tomorrow I have two things to do. First get the bike serviced and then try and locate Rahul Bhatia, my suicidal client. His phone call is still simmering on the back burner of my brain.

Next morning, a waft of fresh cool breeze enters as I open the door and walk out of the room to look at my motorcycle standing outside. 700 kilometres and the machine has performed well; doesn't really need servicing, just a wash. I've been topping up the engine oil and that's about all the care it has needed. I take out the tool kit and spanner, tighten the nuts and check the cables—all OK. I decide to skip the mechanic and go looking for Rahul.

This is my second visit to Nagpur. The first was too long ago for me to remember any details except that I had escorted an elderly blind rich man who had wanted to visit the missionary school and church here. My first impression of modern day Nagpur is of friendliness. The people here are polite and helpful and seem to love their food. Restaurants abound. I walk into one called Haldiram (recommended by Suresh) and break my day's fast with a pair of spicy *samosas* and a glass of sweet *lassi*. Feeling fortified enough I begin my quest for Rahul. I have no idea where he lives. But I know his father runs a sports-trophy business. I ask the waiter if he knows where I could buy a sports trophy, which for some reason makes him smile. He walks away with my payment, casting a sly backward glance. Maybe sports trophies mean something else in his slang. Out on the road, another more normal gentleman says I should go to Central Bazaar where, he says, 'There are many types of many shops.' An auto rickshaw takes me to Central Bazaar and stops in front of a large sports trophy shop. I walk into it. Wooden cupboards all around display huge, medium and small trophies made of silver, brass and steel, mounted on blocks of polished wood. There is an elderly man at the counter. I tell him I am looking for Rahul Bhatia's shop. Does he know where it is?

'I am Bhatia, Rahul is my son.' But why was I asking?

Taken by surprise at hitting pay-dirt so quickly, I told him I was from Pune and disclosed the reason I was looking for Rahul.

'Oh. So you are the one!' I didn't quite know how to interpret his reaction. He didn't sound particularly upset or angry. In fact, he was smiling. From Rahul's descriptions of his father, I had pictured a big dominating, bully kind of guy but here instead, was a frail and gentle looking man who looked rather lonely sitting alone in his huge shop. He came out from behind the counter and shook my hand. He then dragged a plastic chair for me.

'Glad to meet you, sir. Please take a seat.'

I was rather surprised by his hospitality. The 'sir' was reassuring.

'Rahul is not in Nagpur. He's in Nigeria working as a sales manager for Honda's Lagos office. But he is coming back in two months. He wants to settle down. In fact, we are now looking for a girl for him to marry. I have to thank you for all this.'

I listened to Mr Bhatia recount how much he had tried to get his only son to take over his thriving sports trophy business. How frustrated and angry he had become when Rahul refused to come work with him in the shop. How his blood pressure had increased due to all this stress. How he had to take pills to calm himself. That was the time Rahul had 'run away' to Pune to see 'some doctor' (me). He had returned after ten days completely changed. He seemed to have a new air of self confidence. He had got himself a job in Nigeria without even asking me and had been away for almost a year.

But during his absence, the father had changed too. He didn't want to lose his son. He had thought it out, discussed it with friends and family and had, knowing his son's obsession with all things automotive, finally agreed to Rahul's proposal to start a Honda sales and service centre.

Ah... So the father had capitulated and the rebel son had won!

A happy ending! Case closed.

I saw no reason to tell him about his son's suicidal

phone call to me and all that had transpired when he was in Pune. Sometimes, it is best to let sleeping dogs lie.

As politely as I could, I extricated myself from the old gentleman's presence and let a rickshaw take me back to my waiting bike.

Having nothing else to do but feed well and rest, I spend the evening in my room, sprawled on an old-fashioned easy chair with the trusty Old Monk by my side musing on the twist in Rahul's story. Personally I was happy that Rahul had taken my advice and broken away from a life he didn't want. It must not have been easy but he had done it and I felt great to have been a catalyst in his effort. How skilfully had I manoeuvred him away from that suicidal moment in the dark park, how deftly had I burnt away his 'problems', etc. I felt like a guru and loved the feeling! I spent the rest of the evening in pleasant self-congratulation and slid into sleep feeling smug...

Nagzira

TODAY I AM riding to Nagzira Wild Life Sanctuary which is 250 kms away. I plan to get there when the gates open at 3 pm. Dear Suresh (who has contacts within the Forest Department) has booked a cottage for me for the one night I will spend there.

Out of Nagpur, onto NH6 again, by passing Bhandara, I take the recommended left turn at Sakoli and ride through an increasingly rustic scenery. I am passing through a potters' village where the road is lined with huge heaps of gleaming red clay pots. I spot a potter sitting near his stock and stop to take some pictures. The scene I'm in is like a film set of an idyllic Indian village. The potter is grinning with happiness, displaying dazzling teeth. Two women carry brass pots on their hips. A collection of beautiful mud huts with golden thatched roofs and a mandatory cow in the barn complete the picture. The women laugh as I gesture to them to stand still for a photo and oblige me momentarily before walking away, bangles tinkling. The potter tells me the women are his sisters and when I ask how many hours they need for water collection, he pauses to think before answering with two of his fingers. He says the river is two kilometres away and they make two trips every day. He is waiting for the truck to come and pick up his pots. There are over a hundred of them stacked in a pile—some adorned with designs, others spouting tiny steel taps.

I take a few more pictures, say good bye to the happy potter and ride on at a snail's pace through the bazaar. Villagers are engaged in unhurried commerce. Everyone must know everything about everyone in such a small community and the bazaar is where they meet for updates. It is a good place for a *chai* and cigarette stop. A bell rings and a roar erupts from the school next door. Excited children begin to pour out of the compound. A few run to an old lady sitting near the gate with a collection of bottles and packets spread out around her. She is the snack lady selling toffees, peanuts, tamarind, dry berries and other things that children find irresistible. Nearby, a shrivelled old man is busy serving kids who have opted for his speciality which is crushed ice-balls pressed around a stick of bamboo and drizzled with red syrup.

Out of the village, back on the state highway, patches of bright green fields slowly fade out with the huge trees lining both sides getting denser by the minute. A signboard tells me I am now only an hour away from the sanctuary. The road is narrow but in good condition and there is no traffic. A flock of egrets suddenly take off from the edge of a small pond on my right and flutters close overhead as I purr away.

Soon I am at the gate of the sanctuary. A board informs me that the park will open at 3 pm. I have an hour to wait. A large village borders the sanctuary and there are many people loitering around. They all look rather rough, wild and colourful. A few shacks are littered around the main gate.

I park the bike near a tea shop and order a cup. Men sitting under a tree nearby are playing cards for money. Sipping my tea, I watch. It's a rather simple game they are playing. Each player contributes Rs. 5 to the kitty and is dealt five cards face up. A young man is tabulating scores. The first one to reach a total of 200 wins it all. Periodically, someone gets up to walk to the tin and bamboo shack nearby which is selling *arak*, a strong smell of liquor pervades the air.

3 o'clock comes and the park is open for visitors. I seem to be the only one today.

The man behind the ticket window, whom I can't clearly see, tells me motorcycles are not allowed in the park (for obvious reasons) and I'll have to leave it somewhere outside. I'll have to hire a jeep and a guide who will take me to my cottage which is three kilometres inside the jungle.

He directs me to the single Scorpio SUV presently available. A short stocky man is standing next to it looking at me. I walk up to him and ask if he will take me. He says he is both the driver and guide and since it's not yet tourist season, he will charge me only Rs.1800. With a bit of bargaining, we settle for a Rs.1500 contract which will include transportation to my allotted cottage inside the sanctuary, a two-hour drive through the jungle at dawn and a return back to this gate. I tell him about my problem with leaving the motorcycle unattended and he solves it by saying I can park it in his courtyard. His house is nearby. I ride through the wicker gate and past the fence of hay and bamboo and park my baby in a corner, next to the chicken coop. Ishwar, my driver and guide awaits me outside, engine purring softly. I cover the loaded motorcycle with its tarp and take only my small food bag which has everything I will need for a night's stay—dry fruits, water, rum, cigarettes, torch and the tube of mosquito repellent.

The twenty-minute drive provides time for my mind to adjust to the ambience of an Indian jungle. Ishwar is an immediately likable young man who seems to genuinely love the jungle and is certainly quite knowledgeable about the flora and fauna. I Ie has a gentle voice and is reeling off name after name of the various birds and animals that live in this 150 square kilometre jungle. I have a feeling this is going to be a great experience. For one, it is nice to get off the bike and relieve the brain of the need for total

concentration on the road. It is soothing to let my eyes
wander all around rather than focus just straight ahead.

Ishwar has been working as a guide here for a decade
now and has tip-of-the-tongue answers to my questions. I
ask the most obvious one : 'Tiger *hai kya*?' He says there
are four of them, one with two cubs. There are also
leopards, bears, buffalo, hyenas and plenty of deer of all
sizes. I am suddenly very glad I'm not riding my open bike
on this road. I get my pack of cigarettes out but Ishwar
stops me from lighting up. Smoking is not allowed inside
the jungle. I vow to not smoke for the next 20 hours.

The cottage was one of six, spread in a wide spacious semi
circle around a football-sized open patch of land with a
garland of upright Ashoka trees all around. Beyond
bordered the dense foliage of the jungle with a ten foot
wide red dirt road disappearing into it. Groups of white
furred and long tailed langur monkeys sat scattered around
the area. An eagle's shrill trilling call penetrated the silence
like laser.

The cottage itself was a simple affair. Just a room with
a bed overhung with a mosquito net and a tiny but
adequate toilet. No electricity, sorry. Ishwar brought me
dinner from the canteen. *Dal* and rice which I spiked with
sips of the rum I carry in my hip flask. I spend the evening

sitting out on the concrete threshold of my cottage door, a candle flickering behind me, inside the room, making the shadow of my head dance on the earth in front. The darkness around is otherwise total. None of the other cottages show any signs of occupation. I hope Ishwar is around somewhere nearby. I call out his name loudly only to be answered by a frog who croaks me a semblance of moral support. Fireflies continue to revel in the dark– oblivious to my building feeling of self-concern.

It strikes me that sitting outside my cottage, in the open in the middle of a real jungle might still be okay if it was the middle of the day. The same enacted in pitch blackness is pushing it a bit. Suddenly I become very afraid, hastily withdraw inside and latch the door. Maybe right now a tiger is using his acclaimed senses to locate what to him must be the lone eatable tourist in the territory? I begin to imagine disaster scenarios which all end in me being eaten.

This night my fear is primal. To the tiger, I will just be food. It won't matter to him who I am or whom I know. The animal will have no thought to spare for my caste, creed, colour, or character. I look at the flimsy latch on the warped wooden door which even a large rat could push open and feel a spurt of adrenalin rush through my body. My nerves are tingling with thrill but not of a pleasant kind. I'm in the throes of paranoia. I recollect Ishwar telling me that there are just four tigers in this 150 square kilometre park. Let's say two of them have already eaten their Sambar dinner. Unlike us humans, animals don't overeat. I for one have never seen an obese tiger on any of those Nat Geo documentaries. That reassures me a bit but still leaves two possibly hungry tigers on the prowl and that's two too many!

Right then, the silence outside is shattered by the sound of a sharp bark followed by a rustle of shrubs. Barking deer? I've read too much Jim Corbett to ever forget that barking deer signal the arrival of the big cat. My glands send in a fresh surge of their remaining stock of adrenalin. This can't go on. I need help! I want to yell my way out of my mind-lock (à la Osho) but caution myself against making any loud sounds and attracting the attention of the Terrifying Two. My only option now is to be brave and sip my remaining rum as silently as I can. My nightmare is a huge tiger biting into my stomach and being pleasantly surprised by the taste of Old Monk much like a rum-filled Swiss chocolate!

When I wake up and open the door, the world doesn't look scary at all. It looks magical. I am not going to turn poetic although the setting well warranted verse. Virgin rays of the just risen sun flash through gaps in the foliage. Around me are birds of all feathers—some flying with purpose; others flitting about just for the joy of it.

Yesterday's monkeys are back, spread across the grounds. One group approaches me to check out if I have any tit-bits for them. I can relate to this desire; I am quite hungry myself. Last night's fear must have cost my body extra calories!

'*Salaam, sahab*,' a voice calls from somewhere behind me and for a nano second, I think the langurs are talking but when I turn around I find that the source of the greeting are two teenage boys each carrying a pail and a broom. After twelve hours of aloneness, I am indeed glad to see someone of my species. I greet them back and follow them into my room which they mean to clean. As I ask them where they're from, I notice one of them has painted his toenails a gaudy red. Ignoring the various connotations that this observation triggers in my brain, I learn that they are from nearby Umajhari and work as cleaners for the Forest Department. Every day they walk to work through the forest. With last night's fearful experience still fresh in mind I ask them about what wildlife they encounter. 'Well,' says the red-toed one and goes on to name just about every animal named in the information brochure that came with the ticket. They've spotted the big cats many times and of course they are scared. Once, a *barasingha* (twelve-horned stag) had charged at them.

'He must have mistaken you for a *hiran* (deer),' retorts his friend and then both supress giggles at their private joke as they sweep the dust off the floor. Job quickly done, they stand still in the age-old manner of someone hoping to be tipped. Another '*Salaam, sahab,*' is uttered almost in unison and the two move out of my life, never to be seen again.

Half an hour passes before Ishwar drives up in his SUV with a thermos full of welcome coffee. My electric tea maker has been of no use here. I pack up my meagre belongings and jump in next to Ishwar to begin the safari. We enter the jungle through the red mud road and the cottages disappear from view. Trees crowd us on both sides and huge anthills, some eight feet high, appear at regular intervals. The jungle has many internal roads but all look the same to me. I see a huge head of a buffalo staring at me with what seem to be angry eyes from between the trees. Then our progress is halted by a log fallen across the road and Ishwar has to get down and pull it out of the way. I stay inside the vehicle not daring to venture out. The buffalo is nearby and who knows what else? I miss the safety of a National Geographic documentary.

A group of big and small *chital* in a small clearing, a ten-foot python curled up around a tree stump, another wild buffalo's behind and that was the end of the ride. No tigers but I'm not too unhappy about that. We stopped at the canteen for a quick breakfast of *idli-sambhar* and coffee and were at the sanctuary gate by 10 am. Ishwar drove me back to my bike. I paid and thanked him and was soon back on the same country road I was on two days ago.

This time though it seems totally different. The day

before it was new and unknown and surprise had awaited me at every turn.

I'm passing the potter's village again and sight a group of maybe a dozen boys and girls who are all walking to school. Most of them are in their uniform of white shirts and blue shorts or skirts. Many are barefoot. As they turn around at the sound of my slow moving motorcycle, I don't know what comes over me because I raise the visor of my helmet and shout, '*Aaz Shala Baand*,' (School Closed Today. Holiday Today), causing an excited buzz amongst the suddenly energized young crowd. The entire bunch stops in mid-stride and begins chattering over this piece of good news. I try to mentally become a ten-year-old who has just learnt that a boring school day is now a holiday. As I pass them and lower the helmet's visor, I hear my late father's voice ask me why I've just committed a completely needless act of antisocial mischief. Having no rational answer, I just keep mum until the voice inside my head fades away, masked by the unceasing hum of the highway which is now taking me to Raipur, the capital of the state of Chhattisgarh.

A group of women is blocking the road ahead and crowding around the driver's side of a car they've stopped. As I slow down and stop at a distance behind the car, I see that they are not women at all but young men wearing saris and bangles with stuffed cotton for breasts. They are demanding money from the driver who argues with them before throwing some change and hastily moving on.

Then it is my turn. All six come and crowd around me, clapping their hands like *hijras* are known to do.

Still astride the bike, I pull out my wallet to take out a ten rupee note to give them when one of them snatches my wallet and runs. I try to grab him but find myself holding a fake breast while he stands away from me, blouse exposed, my wallet in his hands, grinning.

I get off the bike slowly and put it on its stand. Then with an abrupt movement, I grab at the guy closest to me and stuff the fake 'breast' in my hand, into his blouse before I shove him. I turn to the group and in a severe tone warn them to immediately return my wallet or else... I add a few choice expletives and for a poignant minute, maintain a steady-eyed stare. None of them dares ask me who I am or what exactly it was that I propose to do. They must take me for a police officer or something—which is exactly what I want them to think. They whisper amongst themselves and tell the snatcher to return my wallet and, 'Sahab se maafi mango.' (Ask sahab for forgiveness.)

The wallet is returned along with a collective apology by all six. They are now entreating me not to do anything to them. Having got my wallet back, I drop my authoritarian manner and smile which makes all of them smile back. In a softer voice I ask them what all this was about.

'Hum kya karein, sahab, aise hi thoda paisa milta hai,' one of them starts explaining and goes on to tell me that they are all from Gurupur and are not really *hijras*. But this is a good way to make money. 'Everyone gives us money. Some even ask us to bless their children.'

'So how much do you make each day?' I ask the best dressed amongst them. The six of them take in around a thousand rupees which is their target for every day and which they share equally. They get more during festivals.

I am fascinated by their enterprise and adopting a non-judgemental tone, ask them more questions. They have sensed my interest in their lives and seem to have lost their apprehensions about punishments I had threatened to dish out. They now seem anxious to tell me all about themselves, interrupting each other like excited children, bragging. They are no longer apologetic about their business. The well dressed one who is doing most of the talking, says it is *bahut mast kam* (very good work). It's all his idea. He had lived in Kolkata for two years and seen groups of *hijras* make a lot of money simply by walking into shops and clapping their hands. That's when the idea had struck him. He tweaks his thumb and middle finger as he says this. Why not export the idea to Gurupur? No investment necessary—just borrow your mother's (or wife's) sari and you're in business. Ingenious. He had spent five hundred rupees from his last salary buying cheap trinkets, oversized bangles, and make up. When he returned to Gurupur he got to work. There was no dearth of unemployed young men who were anxious to join him but he only needed five. He informs me that traditionally, *hijras* move in groups of six, the reason they are called '*chakkas*' ('sixes'). They all had to let their hair grow and get their ears pierced. 'But these days many men do that anyway.' I compliment him on his entrepreneurship and give him and the others a ten rupee note each. That done, I shake each of the six bejewelled hands thrust at me and wishing them all a successful professional life, I get astride and ride on.

Back on NH6, I make fast progress and am in Raipur before dark. My wife's maternal uncle lives in Devendra Nagar and is expecting my call. He says Vijay, his son, will meet me at the railway crossing and guide me home. I've never met Vijay but he has no difficulty in spotting me. After all, how many old men with loaded, out-of-state Royal Enfields must there be in Raipur? It's quite crowded around here so after only a perfunctory greeting, Vijay asks me to follow his scooter which begins to wind its way through crowded bazaars where I have to make a special effort not to let my bulging luggage nudge any pedestrians. We are entering a densely populated area with tiny double storey houses closely packed together. Space is at a premium here. Vijay turns into a side street and stops in front of a house which is in comparatively better shape. It constitutes two small rooms, one stacked on top of the other. He opens the gate and signals for me to bring the motorcycle in and park it. 'It will be safe here,' he says. By this time the entire family is out to greet me. *Mamaji*, in his six-foot frame, is still looking strong at seventy. His two sons and their wives, his five grandchildren all line up and take turns touching my feet, leaving me no option but to bless them. On the road, I had forgotten that I was actually a fifty-seven-year-old man but here and now with my wife's relatives touching my feet, I must act in tune with their expectations.

What follows is two days of being treated like royalty. *Mamaji* says I need rest and a little 'fattening up' for the ride ahead. He has heard from Meena that I like mutton *biryani* preceded by two inches of Old Monk and all arrangements are in place. I am to sleep in the upstairs room. That would mean the ten of them would sleep cramped in this small downstairs room (which is also the kitchen, study room for the children and a corner reserved for God and TV). My protests are of no avail. They say I have no say in the matter.

For two days, I do nothing but eat delicious food and sleep long hours and by the end of it, I am rejuvenated and ready to get back on the road.

The next day, I'm up by 5 am. The bike is loaded, ready to take off by 6. Only *Mamaji* is awake to see me off. His final words are cautionary. He warns that I'll now be passing through the Naxalite Belt and should take care. Bad things are known to happen to travellers on the road I am about to take. 'Good things too,' I am tempted to retort but wary of sounding disrespectful, I make do with a *Namaste*.

Dhaba Guru

I AM NOW riding through a dry and dusty plain sparsely dotted with Babul—the hardy tree which grows in the most arid of terrains. It is near noon, the sun is blazing on the road which stretches straight ahead of me. It is not wide enough to allow much space between the two-way traffic. Trucks pass me and add diesel fumes to the hot and dusty air which finds its way into my nose.

I have just enough time to raise the visor of my helmet before the sneeze erupts.

Ah…Achhhoooo!

Automatically, my right hand lets go of its hold on the throttle, covers my face and I hear myself say a reflexive 'excuse me' which then makes me feel silly because there is no one around to do the excusing. No one, except a stray dog, who sprints to chase me for half a minute before stopping and beginning to pant as I get my right hand back on the throttle and speed on.

The heat around is enough to dehydrate dog or man and when I spot the road sign announcing the existence of Prem Dhaba just a kilometre ahead, where travellers are being promised some 'Testy Food', I decide to take them up on the offer.

Prem Dhaba is set a distance away from the road and is actually just a tin roof supported by a dozen gnarled branches of Babul. I park, free my food bag from its holding straps and walk into the shaded space. Half of this wall-less restaurant is occupied by the kitchen where a middle aged man is stirring up the contents of two large pots bubbling on the wood powered stoves. The other half is where the customers sit and eat—eight of them on a house-full day! I am the lone diner—it's a bit too early for lunch which the cook announces will be ready only after an hour. I ask him if I can sit and wait and needless to say, he says of course!

I need to top up the body's evaporated electrolytes which I do by mixing up lemon juice concentrate with salt and powdered sugar and then diluting it with my precious supply of filtered water. I have my own clean glass too. As I sip my drink, a young man of about twenty-five comes into view. He's just got off his bicycle which, if it were a person, would have been labelled schizophrenic. It is half junk-yard and half store. The rear carrier is heaped with metal junk; a twisted, rusted bicycle wheel, a broken metal bucket and all kinds of metal scrap. The rear of his bicycle speaks of the passing of things that were once new, useful and coveted but now not wanted by anyone except a scrap merchant. Depressing!

Beyond the elevated seat, the front of the bicycle is a whole new world, full of promise and gaiety. Shiny plastic containers of various sizes, shapes and colours, gleaming bright in the afternoon sun, are bunched up around the bike's handle.

The chap walks in and sits at the other table. He greets the cook (who responds with a perfunctory nod), then looks at me and greets me with a '*Salaam, sahab*' which I acknowledge with a nod. That's enough encouragement he needs to begin asking me where I'm from and where I am going, what I do for a living and how many kilometres does my bike run per litre of petrol. Not sure whether he knows what a speech therapist is, I tell him I am a '*bolne ka doctor*' (a speech doctor) which starts him off on addressing me as 'doctor *sahab*' from then on. He tells me he is in great difficulty and just doesn't know what to do; his life has become a mess. Could I help him with his problem? I wonder what he means. Is he trying to get some money out of me? But maybe it is not money he's after. The quiver in his voice and the despondency on his face suggest the possibility of a different dilemma. So I ask him what his problem is and get this story for an answer.

'Doctor *sahab*, I am a Brahmin. Ramprasad Hariram from Choubattia village. I was working as a cook in this very *dhaba* but now no one will eat food cooked by my hands and I have become a *kabaadiwala*.' The gist of it was that about a year ago he had got a local girl pregnant. She was the daughter of a low caste cobbler and his Brahmin family had threatened him with excommunication if he married her. The pregnant girl filed a police complaint and he had been arrested. The police after thrashing him for three days had given him a choice. He could either marry the girl or go to jail for a minimum of seven years. What was he to do? He didn't want to go to jail; he'd heard horrific stories of what happened there. He had taken her to Sambhalpur where they had got married.

But once they had come back to their village, no one from his family talked with him. He was fired from his job as a cook because only Brahmins were allowed to be cooks. He now had to do the 'low-caste' work of exchanging scrap for plastic utensils. It was hard work and he didn't make much, not enough to support his wife and baby daughter. Now his mother-in-law had come to stay with them too—her cobbler husband having died right after the marriage. It was one more mouth to feed. Plus mother and daughter had teamed up against him and become quarrelsome. He was stuck with the 'low-castes' now.

He continued narrating his tale of woe which was beginning to acquire the potential to spoil my lunch which the cook had placed on the table—a bowl of steaming hot *dal* with two buttery *parathas* on a side plate. Ramprasad continued to talk and I was getting a bit tired of him. Letting just a pinch of exasperation seep into my voice, I said, 'Life and problems go hand in hand right to the very end and we all have to handle it the best we can.' I asked him what he wanted from me. 'I want your advice. Tell me what I should do. I'm ready to do anything.' I was about to let my irritation get the better of me but something made me hold on. I told myself to be patient. Here was a distressed human being who, for whatever reason, thought of me as someone who could help him. Couldn't I leave him with a bit of hope?

My meal was finished now and it was time to get back on the road again. I repacked my food bag, paid the thirty-rupee bill and walked out to the bike with plea-faced Ramprasad in tow. How forlorn he looked: bewildered, afraid and overwhelmed. I turned to him and said that I would reveal a very powerful mantra to him which he had to keep to himself and not reveal to anyone or it would lose its power. I then closed my eyes and waited for a nice sounding, meaningless word to compose itself in my mind. 'Dogho' is what came and stayed. I told him he should repeat 'Dogho' ten times each sunrise and sunset and it was guaranteed to bring him good fortune and freedom from all problems of life. He could also say it anytime he was in a difficult situation. I took a pinch of the powdered sugar and asked him to open his mouth as wide as he could and stick his tongue out as far as he could stretch it, then deposited the finely powdered sugar on his tongue, myself blessing him with a few preliminary 'Doghos' to start him off. I cautioned him to keep his tongue out for as long as he could and not swallow the sugar to increase the mantra's power.

While he was preoccupied with not-swallowing, I got astride, kick-started the bike, and left Hariram with a mantra which, if reversed, was also the one we all frequently use.

Time For a Joke?

MONDAY EVENING. HOT summer's day. San Francisco. Buxom blonde Susan, thirty-five, trudges up the stairs to her second floor apartment, holding two heavy brown paper grocery bags in the crooks of both elbows and hand-bag strapped over her left shoulder. Tired. Irritable. Presses bell. No answer even after five attempts. Where the hell was John? Probably doped, sleeping. Phew! That husband of hers! She puts the grocery down and hunts for key from the mess in her handbag. Opens the door and walks in.

Shades are drawn. The room is dark. Incense is thick in the air. John sits on the floor, cross-legged. Eyes closed. Chanting unintelligibly.

'Hey, John!' (twice)

'Shhhh...'

'What're you doin'?'

'Shhhh... Don't disturb me.'

'But what on earth are you doing?'

'Shhhh… Don't shout. I'm meditating.'

'What the hell is that? What are you murmuring?'

'Shhhh… Don't swear. I'm repeating a mantra.'

'What's a mantra?'

'It's a magic word.'

'Sounds like voodoo. Where did you get that from?'

'Shhhh… Talk softly. I got it from an Indian Swami, Gurooo Baba Nath Jee.'

'What does it do?'

'It solves all sorts of problems.'

'Well… Tell me what it is, I can use it. I've got problems too.'

'Uh…huh…,' John nods, 'can't tell you what it is. Guroo Baba Nath Jee said if I told my mantra to anyone, it would shed its power. Then I'd have to pay him another 100 dollars to reactivate it.'

'Gawd… No! You actually paid for it?'

'500 dollars' says John eyes still closed.

'What! You useless, unemployed prick! You paid 500 dollars of my hard-earned money to some Hindoo conman for a useless mumbo-jumbo mantra which you won't even tell me?'

'Guruji said not to share it with anyone or it will lose its power to make my deepest wish come true.'

'That does it! I can't take it anymore.'

Susan rushes to her room, crying loudly. Within five minutes, she's out of the bedroom lugging a suitcase which she deposits outside the open front door. She looks back and yells, 'I'm leaving! I want a divorce! You'll hear from my lawyer,' before slamming the door shut.

A minute after the sound of her clicking heels fades, John
opens one of his two eyes, puts both arms up and exclaims...
'It works!'

Evening is approaching and I begin to look for a place to
park for the night. The signboards inform me that Sohela
is now 20 kilometres away. Soon people, shops and shacks
begin to line both sides of the road.

'Downtown' Sohela is a collection of petrol pumps,
automobile repair workshops, tyre dealerships, *dhabas* and
a number of liquor shops and bars. Many trucks are parked
around. Everyone seems to have either just arrived or
ready to move out. There is an air of temporariness about
this town—no one seems to have the time to care for it.
Everything around looks covered with dust and fixed with
grime.

I ride through the length of the town looking for a
hotel. Instead, I discover a PWD guest house—a
government property built to house visiting engineers
and staff of the Public Works Department. Such PWD
guest houses dot the length and breadth of India and are
usually located on the outskirts of a town. Many have
been built in the early 1950s and possess the old-world
charm of long gone times. I turn right and pause to read
the faded signboard hanging on the rusted gate,

permanently wide open, each of its panels having shed a hinge. The main guest house stands silent on my left. Not seeing anyone around, I ride the short, hedge-bordered gravel path which leads me to a row of three brick and mud huts. I park the bike near the first hut and walk to it. It smells of cow and when I peep into it, the blank face of a black cow stares back at me. After a long day's lonely ride, the indifference in its bovine eyes is disconcerting and I avert my gaze and look around for someone to acknowledge my presence.

Presently, a dark skinned young man walks up to me. He's dressed in faded brown shorts and nothing else. His small build, dark skin and bushy hair gives him a wizened aboriginal kind of look. He is rubbing his eyes with the back of his hand. He has obviously been crying because I can see tears in his reddened eyes. I can't ignore his tears and begin by asking him '*Kya Hua?*' (What happened?) expecting him to tell me some fresh tragic story. The truth turns out to be less dramatic. '*Pyaz kaat raha tha,*' (I was slicing onions) he says. My concern for his emotional wellbeing fades and I ask if a room is vacant. He says the entire guest house is vacant and I can stay if I get permission from the police. The police station is a kilometre back into town. He says I should meet Inspector Saha. '*Kurkurey ne bheja bolo.*' (Tell him Kurkurey has sent you.) I kick start the bike for what I hope will be its last ride for the day, and head back towards town.

The Sohela Police Station is a one acre campus with

three single-storey buildings surrounded by many large Pipal trees. Under one such tree, a group of five men stand huddled around someone who is sitting on a metal chair. I park the bike and walk up to the group to discover that the seated gentleman is a bald, elderly professional petition writer currently scribbling away at a frantic pace on light green legal paper. I wait till he finishes his sentence before audibly clearing my throat. This makes him look up. When I ask him where I can find Inspector Saha, he points his finger at the farthest construction, shakes it three times to make sure I've got it and then goes back to his script. The crowd again closes over him.

I walk towards Inspector Saha's office wondering if it is safe to leave my loaded bike unattended. There are people loitering all over the place and the possibility that some of them are genuine thieves cannot be completely ruled out. But would they dare to steal in a police station, which as it turns out is also a jail? I lock the bike and ascend the two steps to the raised platform of a corridor. The first room I enter is a 20x20 feet hall housing three container-sized holding cells which have bars for doors. Two of these cells are vacant but the third one has a lone occupant squatting on the stone floor with his arms wound tightly around his legs. He is a tribal and looks shrivelled—just skin and bones with the haunting eyes patented by the dispossessed of this earth. A group of men stand in a corner. In one section of the room I spot a portly constable sitting at a desk, shuffling a sheaf of forms. I approach him and say I want to meet Saha *sahab* extending my visiting card. He takes it into the adjacent room which I presume is the inspector's office and returns to tell me to wait for a few minutes as he pulls up a vacant plastic chair for me. I plonk myself on it, relieved to be sitting on something that doesn't move. My brain, hyper-stimulated by ten hours on the road, needs a few minutes of rest. I close my eyes and blank out all thoughts. My two minutes of meditation. I open my eyes to find the constable as well as the prisoner staring at me with avid interest. The constable then asks me the usual 'where-what-who' questions and appears to be quite happy with my answers. He is a friendly fellow. I ask him what the man in the cell has been jailed for.

'*Yeh saala? Murghi chura raha tha, hotel ke peeche se. Abhi abhi pakad ke laya hoon.*' ('This bastard? He was stealing a hen from behind the hotel. I have just caught him.') Caught and likely to be thrashed for stealing a hen, right now, the culprit himself looks like a chicken trapped in a cage.

An electric bell rings. The constable goes into the inspector's room and returns to tell me Inspector Saha will see me now. I get up and walk into the inspector's office. He is in his chair and there are three tribal men standing around him. The inspector is saying something to them in a language I don't understand. His tone is stern and firm and as he concludes, all three nod in unison and walk out. I wonder what trouble they are in. Stealing a goat? The inspector then turns and looks at me with a deadpan face and raises his eyebrows. I introduce myself, briefly tell him about my journey, then make my request for the room at the PWD Guest House. He has my visiting card in his hands and is studying it as I talk. He then looks up and exclaims in Hindi, *'Biswas nahi ho raha hai!'* (I can't believe it!). He looks amazed. I wonder if my face resembles a wanted man's? 'This is really a mmm...mm...mi... miracle... So many years I'm looking for speech therapist. You see, I am suffering from stammering.'

'Oh,' I respond with relief, mentally switching from being on the defensive into my therapist's mode. He tells me he stammers a lot, especially when he is speaking to his superiors or someone in authority. I ask him a few questions and offer a few standard suggestions on how he can improve his speech fluency. Our 'therapy session' continues for half an hour, embellished with welcome tea and biscuits.

All this while, a crowd has collected at the inspector's door. It's time to taper off the session. I don't want to slow down the wheels of the Law of the Land (LoL). I tell him he can be in touch with me on telephone for follow-up guidance. I start to get up but he beats me to it and escorts me to the door. I can see he is very appreciative of my advice. The crowd has been watching us and the inspector's deference to me has not gone unnoticed. As Saha and I come out of the room, the crowd parts for us making me feel like Moses. Inspector Saha now insists he wants to pay me my consultation fee. 'Aphter all, you have giben me bery baluable adbice,' he says and I notice the tribal who is still sitting in his frozen hunched up position in the lock up.

I feel a certain empathy with him. How lost and vulnerable he looks. My own jail experience was a picnic compared to his.

In 1968, I was eighteen and we were refugees living in a low-income chawl in Bombay. Our neighbours were newspaper vendors, paan-shop owners, factory workers, and their children were the friends I grew up with. Those were tough times for everyone. Money was scarce and frustration ripe.

Into this scene moved in a politically aware cartoonist who launched a campaign against the 'outsiders' in Bombay (sorry, Mumbai) who were taking jobs away from the local Maharashtrians. His platform was a fortnightly published Marathi magazine which kept up a tirade against South Indians who had migrated to the city in search of work. Rumours and other insinuations began to find willing believers. It was only a matter of time before it all blossomed into a full blown riot.

The day of the riot, a Sunday, had dawned innocently enough for my mother to have caught an early train to Matunga (a suburb of Mumbai, housing mainly South Indians) where she was visiting a dying relative.

By noon, gossip of shops being looted by riotous mobs began to filter into our neighbourhood and by afternoon eye witness accounts changed rumour to fact. Papa said I should go wait for Mother at the railway station. This was 1968 and phones were rare. Only doctors and high government officials had them. We didn't and consequently there was no way to know which train she was coming on. Nevertheless, I ventured out feeling all grown-up and responsible—a first-time shining knight venturing into danger to protect his mother. Also I wanted to see what a riot looked like.

Gokhale Road which led to the Thane Railway Station smelt different today. It was deserted except for a few hurrying passersby. No traffic. Shops had pulled down their shutters. Fear was in the air. Someone yelled, 'Pudhe zaoo nako,' (Don't go ahead) but I hastened my steps and turned right on Station Road.

And there it was... the riot.

There were no less than fifty men varying in age from fifteen to fifty but all caught in a common frenzy of aggression. Some carried six-foot long iron bars and had handkerchiefs tied around their faces. They ran around wild-eyed, yelling, 'Jai Maharashtra!' and looking for targets to bash up. Three teenagers stood near an open truck full of broken bricks and were enthusiastically supplying their friends with ammunition. Street lamps were being broken and some shops had been set afire, while others were in the process of being looted. The post-office was blazing away. The clanging bells of fire engines, the sirens of approaching police, tear gas canisters exploding—it was all very exciting to my eighteen-year-old self and I wanted a closer look.

Suddenly the action heated up. A large blue police bus drove into the crowd. Twenty tough looking SRPs (State Reserve Police) rushed out and began beating up everyone who came within the reach of their yard long truncheons.

You can well imagine what happened after that, but I'll tell you anyway. I stood where I was and got caught and was beaten up! Heavy hands landed all over me with thuds akin to the sound of Tendulkar's bat as he hit Shane Warne for all those sixes. A couple landed just above my occiput. It's amazing how little it hurt at first. For the first minute, all one felt was a sort of dull heaviness, no pain. And then the swelling built up to an impressive size and started to throb.

Those days, I was a medical student and very proud of my Topiwalla National Medical College identity card. I remember showing it to the inspector who (possibly because he had been hit with a stone and was sporting a large strip of white plaster-dressing for a bleeding cut near his right eye-brow), instead of being impressed as I had hoped he would be, tore it in two and threw it back at me, mouthing some unprintables. Understandable in retrospect, but rather upsetting for me at that time.

We were driven, all 119 of us, in a convoy towards Thane Central Jail. My co-passengers were in an exuberant mood, high on adrenalin, yelling their slogans. They were having such fun while I sat glumly in a corner, physically and mentally beaten up. What had hurt me most was how the inspector had failed to differentiate between an upright citizen (me) and common rioters. Did I really look like a hooligan?

We were all pushed into a large hall which must have doubled as a dining area because there were many steel tables and plastic chairs spread around. Apparently this was to be our jail. There was no room for so many people in the main jail.

Smarter fellow inmates quickly commandeered all tables to use as beds. I spent a disturbed night sitting in a corner, nursing my injured head and wondering how to get news of my predicament to my father.

Next day, I woke up amidst festivities. Film songs played on a radio somewhere. People outside vied for views of us—we were heroes to them. Cups of tea and packets of food were thrust at us. I caught hold of an extended hand and pulled at it until the owner's face was against the upright iron bars. He said he was honoured I had asked him to go to my house to let my dad know my whereabouts.

Inside the hall a short, stocky guy hopped up on one of the tables and began to address a dozen others standing in a circle around him. I tuned in to what he was saying and realized that the fellow was actually conducting a short-course on 'How to Burn a Bus in Two Minutes.' He was advising his eager protégés against igniting the petrol-tank which, he said, was well-insulated. Instead, they should set fire to all the four tyres because once it catches, rubber burns easily and has a nice, obvious, thick, odious, black smoke, visible for blocks. The burning tyres would ultimately heat up the petrol-tank enough for it to explode while, at the same time, allow them enough time to run away and avoid injury or arrest! 'Brilliant!' proclaimed the impressed yokels and possibly a new leader was born.

Next day, I was released. The message to my father had

indeed been delivered. He came to the jail with Mr Pradhan, BA, LLB and bailed me out.

I came back to my chawl in a tonga, accompanied by my father and a beaming Mr Pradhan. Cries of, 'Munna zindabad!' rented the air ('Munna' was my pet name). There was a sizable crowd all around us. My friends now looked at me with renewed respect, tinged with envy. 'Maharashtra saathi turungaat gela!' ('He went to jail for Maharashtra!'), they yelled with fanatic fervour and I floated on cloud nine! After all these years, I'd finally made it to the top!

A week after the riot, entire families in the neighbourhood were going about dressed in the latest fabrics from the newly opened (and looted) Raymond Woollen Mill's showroom. Imagine, if you can, the sultry, sweaty heat of Bombay and everyone clothed in pants of blue wool, shirts of blue wool, skirts, blouses, bed-spreads, even curtains made from the exact same thaan (or roll) of looted cloth which sons had procured for their hitherto half-naked kin!

And the Dinkars (the nice family next door), who, under normal circumstances, couldn't afford to buy even peanuts, were suddenly eating almonds and walnuts which their sons had snatched from the shelves of the nearby Sweet-Corner, a shop owned by a South Indian. Within a week's time, entire families in Surya Niwas became rosy-cheeked and healthy. Viva la revolution!

Back to the welcome I got from my chawl mates the day I returned from jail. I was a hero. My father quickly slunk away from the scene. Me? I was in no hurry. I was having a great time, trying to soak it all in. Someone even paid the tonga fare. My shirt torn, my footwear missing, but with euphoria in my heart, I was flying high. Eager hands assisted me back to earth. I felt precious.

My celebrity status lasted just about as long as Bitiya Dinkar's looted pistachios. Soon, the riot became old history for everyone else except me. I had to attend court every fifteen days for over a year and a half. My charge-sheet said I had set fire to the post office! Privately, the policeman (who was actually quite a friendly sort of fellow) confessed to me that of course I had done nothing of that sort but they had to accuse me of something. He revealed they had been ordered to arrest 150 people and had actually fallen short of the district collector's target by thirty-one!

But this story has a happy ending. The Maharashtra Government soon got tired of it all and withdrew the cases against all of us. The politicians had moved on in search of new targets. The South Indians of Mumbai had played out their value as an election issue.

Now back to the police station in Sohela with the caged *murghi-chor* (chicken thief).

'How much does a hen cost?' I ask the inspector.

'Hen? You want chicken for dinner? No problem, sir.'

I say no, I don't want chicken for dinner. But since he insists on paying me my consultation fee, I tell him it is the price of the hen the jailed prisoner has been accused of stealing. I want the inspector to let the miserable man out of jail. He listens to me then calls out to the policeman I was talking to earlier, and asks if an FIR has been recorded for the *murghi-chor*. No it hasn't yet. 'Ssss… *saale ko cho…chodd do,*' (Release the bastard) he orders the policeman. The door to the cell is unlocked and pulled open. The man inside embraces himself tighter and doesn't move. The policeman yells a few more times, then drags the man out of the cell. 'These tttt…tri…tribals like jail. Bhere else can they get phree roof and *roti*? They are bery bery happy in jail,' the inspector tells me. The released prisoner, confirming the inspector's statement, does look offended as he is pushed into the wide friendless world outside. I imagine him cursing me in choicest tribalese— damned do-gooders! Just when he thought he was fixed for the night.

The same policeman (who seems to be the only help around here) then leads me out. I can see he thinks I must be someone important to have been able to free a prisoner. Even his boss had called me 'sir'. I walk towards my bike, mount and wait for my escort, expecting him to hop behind me but he has his own motorcycle and gestures for me to follow him back to the guest house. At the gate, he honks impatiently until Kurkure appears, then tells him to take good care of me since I am *sahab's* friend, then salutes me and leaves. That impresses Kurkure who enthusiastically helps me unload my saddle bags and cart them up the seven broad stone steps of the house leading up to a broad outside porch. I follow him into the room. It has a bed in the middle of it. All furniture is old wood, probably a remnant of the Raj. Every exposed surface is covered by a film of dust—hardly surprising with the highway running so close by.

I unpack, wash the highway off my face and discard my sweat-stained riding clothes for crushed but clean ones. Refreshed, I walk out and stroll around the house amongst old banyan trees which are alive with the sounds of hundreds of screeching parakeets. Dusk comes and day turns into night. When I return to the room, I see it has been dusted and the bed now wears a clean sheet. Kurkure has read my mind and brings in a jug full of water and a glass which is all the companionship my hip flask needs. An old guy sipping Old Monk in an old house... That should count for something!

Kurkure brings in a chicken and rice dinner and even offers to get me some ice-cream which I decline. I follow my dictum of early lights-off and slide into bed. I'm facing a wall which lights up every time a truck passes on the adjacent highway. Also, there's the sound of grinding gears and an occasional ear-shattering air-horn. None of this audio-visual assault on my senses succeeds in denying me a deep and relaxing sleep.

Early next morning, I put my tea-maker to use, then go walk about the dark backyard sipping tea. There is a faint breeze and the trees are humming. Bats with 2-foot wide wing spans flutter sounding like periodic drum beats. I peep into the barn and smell the cow. I wish her a good morning and predictably get no response. I walk over to Kurkure's shed and hear him snoring rhythmically.

As soon as it is light, I load the motorcycle and ride out of the PWD guest house and get back onto an already busy NH6. Trucks carrying iron ore dominate the traffic. I am headed to where they are coming from—the mining district of Keonjhar in North Orissa.

Heat and dust keep me company along a fast moving highway which has now brought me to the patch of forest on the outskirts of Keonjhar town. It is a hilly road and the trees offer welcome shade from the sun. I spot a *dhaba* in a small clearing on my left, slow down, stop, put the bike on its stand and go sit on the single plastic chair next to a wooden rope bed on which sits an elderly Sikh gentleman with a flowing white beard, sipping tea with audible rustic slurps. A man comes out of the *dhaba* and stands around saying nothing. He's waiting for my order. He looks rather glum and when I tell him I want *chai*, he turns around and walks away without even an ok.

After a few minutes of wait, he returns holding a glass half-full with tea which he puts in my hand again, without a word. After he has gone, just to make conversation I ask the *sardarji* what is wrong with the *chai*-guy. He says everyone around here is that way. '*Saale hastey hi nahi,*' (No one smiles) he says in a hearty loud voice and a broad grin as if to compensate for the joylessness on the tea server's face. I ask him where he's from. 'Punjab.' He points to a new truck parked off the other side of the road and says he owns it. 'I'm going back to my Ludhiana with the iron ore.' He has been doing it for forty years, one round trip a week. Tea done, I get ready to leave. As I wish him goodbye, he cautions me to be careful in this area. There are *'harami log'* (bastard people) who could shove a knife into you! *'Churra maar dengey,'* he says, stabbing me three times with an imaginary dagger. The matter-of-fact manner in which he says this is oddly reassuring. Guys get knifed. So what?

For the next hour, as I manoeuvre the last 20 kilometres of the road to Keonjhar, I play out a mental scenario where a large knife has just been shoved into my gut. Wonder how that would feel...

Even if I live to be one hundred and fifty years old, the day I die will be that day's today. Am I ready to die today? Do I know how to die today?

Keonjhar town begins where the forest ends and almost immediately, I come upon a three-storey modern looking hotel standing a distance away from the highway. An impressive six-foot tall turbaned watchman opens the gate and I enter a well maintained garden with the hotel standing in the midst of it. Everything about this place looks expensive. It must cater to executives of mining corporations.

Being on the road for half a month now has done wonders for my appearance. From a fairly decent looking, neatly dressed professional, I have turned into a wild haired, grease coated stubble chinned hobo. Not the typical customer who enters the impressive modern foyer I find myself in. I walk up to the reception where a young man in a red tie and dark coat tells me that the cheapest single costs Rs.3000.

Here I have to confess something about myself. I love to bargain. It's no longer about the money. It's the art of it that excites me. I know I'll take the room, whatever it costs. I'm quite looking forward to some rest and food. This place will provide both. But just for the heck of it, I tell the receptionist that I can't afford to pay so much and ask for a discount.

He asks me to wait and goes away to return with a more senior guy. He's the owner of this hotel and when I tell him about how and where from I've come, he shakes my hand and tells me he owns a 1982 Royal Enfield inherited from his father. He dreams of riding to Ladakh but can't take the time off from his job. He wants to see my bike. On the way to the parking lot, I tell him about my own trip to Khardung La. We continue our talk sitting on the sofas in the foyer. He says meeting me has renewed his own desire to travel like I'm doing, and hopes for me to have a nice stay. A bellboy takes me and my bag to room no. 301.

After days of sleeping in rather rustic rooms, I am now in the midst of 4-star luxury. Room service promises a mutton *biryani* dinner at 8 which gives me just enough time for a bath punctuated with sips of Old Monk. I spend the last hour reliving the day's ride and planning out the next day's route before getting into bed and surrendering to sleep.

A restful night's sleep, an early morning wake-up, a cup of tea, a bit of muscle stretch, a hot bath, a hearty breakfast, a quickly loaded-up motorcycle and I am ready for the 200 kilometres I plan to cover today to Kharagpur where the Indian Institute of Technology is my destination of choice.

I leave Keonjhar at 9 am and by mid-afternoon, I have entered Kharagpur, which at first sight looks like an unkempt shabbily dressed child with a runny nose. I ride through yet another crowded market, smelling fish and turmeric and asking for directions, wind my way towards the IIT campus which is set at a distance from the hustle of the main town. I overtake a cycle rickshaw pulling a cage which at first glance I think is carrying chickens to the slaughter house. Instead of chickens, however, this one is packed with five-year-olds sitting with their shoulders touching. The cage is painted yellow and has 'School for Tiny Tits' written on all sides. Someone must have a spelling problem. I wave and the tiny tots return my greetings with unhesitant enthusiasm.

IIT Kharagpur

IT'S A DIFFERENT scene once I enter the Indian Institute of Technology, Kharagpur campus through one of its many gates. Everything looks cleaner and it is certainly quieter here. Well marked, neat tar roads wind through grottos of various types of trees leading to buildings housing various faculties. I am looking for the Department of Computer Sciences and Engineering where I am to contact Professor Anupam Basu. His name has been given to me by a friend in Pune who knows him 'since childhood'. I'm hoping the good professor will help put me up at their guest house.

Groups of young students, mainly male, are scattered around the roads and the shaded lawns of the sprawling campus. I take the recommended turns on the campus roads and park my loaded bike and enter the lobby of the Computer Sciences building. On the Faculty name board I discover that Dr Anupam Basu is the head of his department. I walk up to his office and find it locked. I walk back to the lobby and ask a passing peon who tells me that Dr Basu is out of town. His secretary might have more information and points to a thin young man sitting behind the reception counter. From him I learn that Dr Basu is currently in New Delhi attending an international conference and will return only after a week. When I tell him my tale, he asks why I hadn't said so before. His boss had told him about me. He thought I'd be younger. 'Motorcycling from Pune? Wow! Welcome to IIT. I am Swapan Chatterjee. Would you like some tea?'

I tell him what I would really like is to get a room to rest for a while. No problem he says and looking up the number in the campus phone book, makes a call then smiles and tells me all is arranged. He gives me directions to the guest house, walks me to my bike and as I am ready to leave says he's a biker too and would like to talk with me after I've rested. There's an IIT Bikers' Club and by coincidence they are meeting today.

The Visveswaraya Guest House is a large building of no particular architectural merit. It is spared from ignominy though, by the large garden that surrounds it. Room 206 on the first floor is just large enough for two narrow beds with only a foot of space between them, but I am not complaining. I was lucky to get in. A board at the reception counter is explicit—the guest house is meant only for 'Authorized Officials'. I try to look 'authorized' as I drag the saddle bags up the stairs to my room to dump them on one of the beds. I lie down on the other and slip into siesta mode.

A knock on the door wakes me up. It is Swapan Chatterjee and another young man with unruly hair whom he introduces as his friend Uttam Sen, also a motorcycle enthusiast. The room is too small for the three of us and my new friends suggest we walk to the nearby open air canteen for coffee. On the way, Uttam says they have a lot of biking enthusiasts on campus who have formed a sort of fraternity. A few of them are waiting to meet me at the canteen. Would I mind talking with them? They've heard about my Ladakh ride book and want to hear me speak about it. Surprised and flattered, I nod my 'Sure'.

The canteen is crowded but space has been reserved for us by the bikers' group. We join them and Uttam introduces me. There are fifteen of them and each tells me his name which I promptly forget. They have many questions to ask—about the bike, the roads, the high altitude—bike-talk amidst servings of *samosas*, sandwiches and coffee. Thoughts are electrical (like radio waves?) and any university campus, full of vibrant thinking youngsters, never fails to charge up my own body's batteries.

Two hours swiftly go by. Then it is exchange-of-mobile-number time before goodbyes are said and everyone disperses.

As I walk back across the campus to my guest house, I recollect the hopes and feelings I had harboured when I was twenty-two—fired up with ambition on the one hand; afraid of not achieving it on the other.

It was tough being twenty-two!

The bike is cutting its way through a dry brown, barren, rocky, dusty road. Fields of green periodically spring up and soothe my eyes. A red-turbaned boy, minding his small herd of goats waves. Lone men clad in saffron robes walk with bags containing all they own; many holding aloft the flags of their faith.

Up ahead I spot five women clad in absolute white, walking ahead of me in single file. I go past them, then stop under a tree about a kilometre ahead which gives me enough time to take care of certain basics and even finish smoking a cigarette before I spot them grow in size as they approach me. I know these are Jain nuns—women who have given up their families and their feminity in search of *nirvana*. They are walking barefoot on the hot asphalt. They all wear half-face masks covering their nose and mouth, *saris* wrapped over their shaved scalps and carry a tiny broom with which to sweep the road ahead.

They present a rather grim picture of extreme abstinence from all the pleasures this life has to offer. Their goal is *nirvana* which is something they seem to be chasing with the zeal of extremists. Their weapon is compassion. They are so non-violent that they don't even want to breathe germs in because then the poor creatures would die. They sweep their pathway because they don't want to step on and kill even the tiniest of life forms. They don't even eat anything that grows underground because it would hurt the bacteria around the roots as the poor plant was pulled out of the earth.

As they walk past, they look at me but there is no change of facial expression. Surely they haven't seen many like me, sitting on a bike in the middle of nowhere. They don't look interested as they go by which does leave me feeling rather ignored.

I mount the bike and wave out as I pass them yet again but none of them show even the slightest response. Maybe they are forbidden by their belief system to wave back. I wonder what's going on in their heads. Many of these are intelligent, educated women from wealthy families who have voluntarily chosen to live in the extreme way they do.

The road is flat and straight and except for a few trucks, there isn't much traffic. I slow down and overtake a tribe of nomadic herdsmen. Entire families with their life's luggage loaded on mules, horses and donkeys walk in a disciplined single file along the left side of the road. The ponies have the hair of their tails shaped in a trendy step cut. The women are attired in colourful saris and seem to favour heavy silver jewellery; each could very well be carrying a kilo of silver in their anklets, bracelets and necklaces. Many have babies in hammocks on their backs. They form the rear of this walking caravan. In front are the men and older boys shepherding a hundred woolly sheep, careful to not let them stray onto the middle of the road. There are half a dozen pie-dogs that seem trained to keep the herd under control. The men are tall and thin and dressed in loose white clothes and a distinct red turban which must keep the heat of the sun off their scalps as they walk the long hot roads of India. They wear brass earrings and silver neckbands and bracelets. Each is carrying a long bamboo shaft resting on his shoulder.

These nomadic herdsmen move from pasture to greener pasture following the rain. There is a tribe of them that comes to an open field near my house in Pune every year just after the heavy rain has subsided. In no time they put up their tents and seamlessly reboot their lives to fit into a new locale. India's laws allow such nomadic shepherd tribes to seasonally use government land for grazing.

A pressurized blast of hot air swerves the bike off its course and I just about manage to prevent it from heading into the culvert that lines the highway. I keep my balance as a huge container truck coming from the opposite direction whooshes past me. That was close! When the adrenalin rush subsides, I think about what could very well have happened. If the near-death experiencers are to be believed, I could right now have been hovering over my body and seeing tunnels of white light! Again, I wonder how it will be to die. But I don't want to die! Don't even want to think about it. I want to live...more...more...more... I try to compose a song with the beat of the engine providing the rhythm. *More...more...more... Life can become a bore, if all I want is more.* I search for rhyming words and the first one that surfaces is sore... *Oh! My butt is so sore...* (which, by the way, it really is.) My mind is in stupid mode and that's all right for a while, so long as I don't encourage it to begin composing songs with lyrics that sound suspiciously similar to some of the crap that gets sung in today's Hindi films. I've been talking to myself for too long. Better shut up and concentrate on the road!

It is near noon as I wind my way eastwards on NH6 which is approaching its own final destination—the big, Bengali metropolis of Kolkata. I'm now on a flyover which is letting me bypass Kolkata and get on to the north-bound NH34. I'm relieved I don't have to ride through the messy metropolis where, reports say, the citizens have yet to agree to certain common rules of traffic management.

The road I'm on is no less crowded forcing me to go much slower than I have been on the fast-paced and wider NH6. For ten days I had been able to ride long stretches at speeds of 80 kmph. That is no longer possible on this road which is now going through Krishnanagar, a suburb of Kolkata. Today, festive-fever has gripped the populace here, and why not? The mother of all festivals is coming. A policeman blows his whistle and I stop. Half the width of the road ahead has been cordoned off for an upcoming *pandal* and traffic is being regulated around it. The *pandal* builders have dug deep holes in the tar road and thick staves of wood are being fixed upright by bare-chested young men who are ramming rocks around the base. Others are unloading wooden planks from a truck. The policeman blows his whistle again and I get moving.

Strikes and Broken Bridges

THE HIGHWAY HAS become a busy thoroughfare. People are everywhere. Shops, hotels, food stalls, doctor's clinics all jostle for space on both sides of the road which is further crowded with handcarts selling sweets, flowers, trinkets, clothes, shoes and everything else that the citizens might need to celebrate the upcoming *puja*. Clay goddesses in various sizes are being mass produced. An old man with his face, hands and clothes smeared with wet grey clay is using a spatula to trim off excess clay around the waist of an 8-foot-tall image of buxom proportions. Another younger man, probably his son, is stirring up red colour in a bucket. Soon each idol will be clothed and painted and decked with jewellery but for now they look like inert grey humanoids, frozen in action, waiting for the breath of life to be puffed into them.

It is near noon as I wind my way northwards on this

crowded highway. The traffic is moving at a snail's pace and, at one point, comes to a complete halt.

'Strike *Hai*,' the truck drivers are telling each other.

Ahead, a crowd of about hundred people is stopping all traffic. Many are carrying placards. They've set up barricades of drums across half the road and protesters have clustered around the other open half and they don't seem to be letting anyone across.

The day is warming up. I take off my helmet and strap it to the luggage, taking care not to let it jut out and possibly hit an already angry agitator. I ask a passerby what it is all about and he replies with a single word, 'Nandigram'.

The Nandigram land acquisition controversy—the newspapers have been full of it all through this year. I've read that the West Bengal government had tried to forcibly acquire land for a chemical-industry complex and was facing severe opposition from the affected people. Six months ago, the agitation had taken a violent turn and fourteen people had died in police firing inciting further violence.

Warily I approach the road block in first gear. A thin young man wielding a stick comes towards me. '*Rasta bondho...rasta bondho...*' He says the road will remain closed till 5 pm. He looks angry and excitable and I need to be careful not to offend him in any way. I decide to surprise him. Making fists with both hands, I repeat what he was saying. '*Rashta bondho...rashta bondho*,' rounding off the words in an imitated Bengali accent. The man and others around him seem taken aback by my unexpected support. I decide to confuse them some more. Standing up on the footrests, I raise my left hand, repeatedly stab the air in front of me with a pointed finger and shout, 'Bhutan...Bhutan,' making my voice sound loud and hysterical. The road-obstructers can't decide how to react to a mad-looking old man shouting something totally disconnected with their current thought stream which is focused on the strike. I slink away before they can get their thoughts organized. With all traffic halted, the road ahead is clear for me to increase speed and let the air cool the engine which has heated up in the slow crawl.

NH34 is now running almost parallel to the India-Bangladesh border and through open farmland, green with growing grain. A small hut with a tea-stall attached appears ahead and looks like a good place to stop. There's no one in the stall but when I peep inside the hut, I see a young woman sitting cross-legged on the mud floor, breast-feeding her baby. She looks up at me just as I avert my eyes. Moments later she comes out unselfconsciously buttoning up the front of her blouse. 'Chai milegee?' I ask to which she nods yes and goes behind the counter to make the tea. She looks quite young couldn't be older than eighteen—which makes me wonder what her story is. A child bride for sure... Should I talk to her? I want to know her story. But would that be fair? Would I be justified in asking a young woman prying questions just so I have another story to entertain myself and tell others? Doesn't that stink of slumdog-tourism? *'No it doesn't,'* somebody else says inside my head. I want to know her story because I want to temporarily transpose myself and imagine what it would be like to have lived a life like hers, or her husband's or her father's.

Maybe that is why we are all interested in the stories of others, especially the drastic ones. So we can vicariously experience what could very well have been our own story but for a quirk of fate.

I manage to keep my curious mouth shut as she brings me a cup which is full to the absolute brim with tea.

A middle-aged man in the brown uniform of the Border Security Force is walking on the road with a small suitcase in his hand. He stops near my parked bike and spotting me, walks into the *chai* shack. He wants a ride to his BSF camp which he says is just 9 kilometres ahead. He's a big man; six-foot tall and close to a hundred kilos in weight. He tells me he is returning from Bihar and has to rejoin duty before 5 pm today. My mobile clock shows it's 4.25 pm already. He's missed his bus and has been walking along the highway hoping to hitch a ride. Can I help? Handling the already loaded bike on this narrow highway with this hunk perched behind, holding his suitcase, would be asking for trouble. I tell him so at which point the child-bride intervenes to inform us both that no buses will ply today because of the Nandigram Bandh. That then leaves me no option but to agree to take the soldier to his post.

On the walkway to the Ajanta Caves

Happy potter on the road to the Nagzira Wildlife Sanctuary

Safron clad wanderer cycling through West Bengal

Ramprasad with his schizophrenic bicycle in Orissa

Durga idols being made in Kolkata

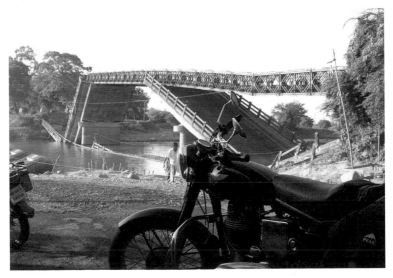

A broken bridge in Bihar

The show must go on. Army lays down a pontoon bridge

Gateway into Bhutan

The Regional Traffic Office, Phuntsholing where they checked
my bike for emissions

GREF Engineers of Indian Army broadening
Phuntsholing–Thimpu Highway

Friendly and fun-loving Bhutanese laugh at the slightest pretext

Lord of all he surveys—Comander Phurpha

In Gedu with the lady who couldn't speak

With the policemen at Chuka Border Post

With Dr Dorji near his hospital in Thimpu

With a monk in Thimpu

Conducting a quick course in Effective
Commuication for the newsreaders of BBS

Key to happiness

Outskirts of Paro

The BSF camp is just off the highway and we make it with a minute to spare. The man says a hurried thanks and jogs away with his suitcase to disappear through the gate. I am back on the highway relieved to be free of the extra load.

I am now approaching Palashi (Plassey) where I hope to find a place to stay. I've read about the famous battle of Plassey in school where the British East India Company had defeated the Nawab of Bengal in 1757. It was the mother of all battles, establishing British rule in India for the next two centuries.

The sun has just set but even the fading light cannot mask the drabness around me. I can see tin-shack shops all along a dusty highway. I've been on the road for ten hours and riding through crowded markets on rough roads has demanded total attention from mind, muscle, ear and eye. Now each one demands rest and listen to them I must. I pull up next to a cluster of shacks, one of which is an auto-mechanic's, and dismount. Three grease smudged young boys are working on a Honda 100 cc which has its innards open. An older man with the body language of a boss interrupts instructing the boys to respond to my query. I've asked him about any nearby hotels and he's said there's one just off the highway on the road leading to Meherpur in Bangladesh.

'Bery lobely hotel,' he emphasises.

But if I'd hoped to be housed in style in any of the *dak* bungalows that the British must surely have built, I am in for quite a disappointment.

This hotel looks anorexic. It is disproportionately thin. Four storeys built on a 1000 square foot plot. I enter the lobby with a tiny reception counter which has just enough space for the man standing behind it. I ask for the deluxe suite and am told I'll have to do with a corner single room on the third floor. He assures me it has a, 'Bery lobely biew'. I have no option but to take his word for it. I hand him the 400 rupees he's quoted and sign the register. He then comes out and helps unload the bike. I follow him up the steep metal stairs, dimly lit by flickering bulbs. 'Low boltage,' explains my guide just as we reach the door of what must be the promised room with a lovely view.

The door swings inside but is prevented from opening fully; the bed is in the way. There is just enough space for us and the saddle bags to get through. The bed occupies most of the room's limited floor space and is clad in faded floral sheets spotted with stains of questionable character. I silently thank Meena for insisting I carry a clean bed sheet for just such contingencies. A small foot-wide window is the room's only redemption. It is too dark to see the view but it is allowing a steady current of cool air into what would have otherwise been a claustrophobic space.

The friendly hotel man switches on the light and says I should park the bike in the lobby for the night. It will surely be stolen if I leave it out. As he goes out, he wants to know if I want anything from the kitchen. 'Nothing,' I say having resolved to not even use the empty glass for the drink I plan to pour as soon as the guy leaves. I'm carrying my own water too. Dinner will be light tonight. Cashews, almonds and raisins lubricated down the gullet by the trusted Old Monk. Eyes heavy with sleep, I trudge down the ill-designed metal steps and roll the bike into the lobby, then trudge up again. That's about all the body can do today. Sleep comes even before I can wish myself a complete Good Ni...

Yesterday, at the guest house in the green IIT campus, bulbuls had woken me with their gentle whistles. This morning it is the high intensity air horns from passing trucks that are doing the job. It is only 5 am but already the day is well lit. I look out of the window to check out the much touted view. Plassey doesn't look shabby from up here. Small bungalows surrounded by many trees stretch away from the highway and in the distance I see a quilted patchwork of fields. Green farmlands are stitched to rectangles of black (where the crop stubs are burnt, post harvest) and shades of brown, of earth recently ploughed. Silvery veins of water crisscross the land. There is no dearth of ground water here. The Bhagirati—a tributary from the Ganges flows west of Plassey while the Mother river herself flows not far from here, towards the east.

Feeling compensated to a degree by the sights, I go about my morning chores and once all is done and my bags packed, I drag them down the stairs to the lobby where I see that my bike has not been sleeping alone. The receptionist is lying spread-eagled on the floor next to her. I try waking him up with a loud 'Hello' and when that doesn't work, have to shake him by the shoulders before he gets up and groggily proceeds to unlock the front door of the hotel. I wheel out the bike, load the bags on, and leave without a backward glance.

The highway has become a 30-foot wide potholed road, coursing its way through a continuous stream of human habitation and catering to heavy two way traffic. I have entered what seems to be a predominantly Muslim area. Green and white are the preferred colours of the buildings here; bearded men and burqa-clad women the norm. I pass mosques with loudspeakers mounted on their *minars*. And then, the traffic chokes up again. Trucks and cars standing still in a long line which suggests another major road block. People around are saying that the army has been called in. Army? Was there some trouble? A riot? No...no...nothing like that. The bridge had collapsed into the river early in the morning and the army has put up a floating bridge.

It takes me careful manoeuvring between vehicles and people to reach the head of the waiting queue, at the edge of a 100-foot-wide river. The collapsed bridge is to my right, its broken spine resting on the slow moving water. I sit on the bike to wait and watch.

In front of me is the pontoon bridge that the army has laid out. 15 feet wide, floating on huge torpedo shaped barrels and ending in a flat steel platform at each end.

Soldiers dressed in dark green are directing traffic which is restricted to one way. I take out my camera and shoot pictures of the broken sections of the concrete bridge which have fallen in a paradoxical victory sign.

One of the soldiers, standing near me is a young Sikh and just to make conversation, I ask him how long the wait would be. His answer surprises me; not what he says but the manner in which he does. Like the inspector in Sohela, this man also suffers from stammering. Amazing coincidence! Impelled to offer him some guidance, I tell him my profession, show him my card and once I am convinced that he wants my help, spend half an hour suggesting how he can improve his speech. This trip, I'm a travelling therapist! This is the first time I've talked to a client sitting on a motorcycle. Arvinder Singh is from Abohar, Punjab. He's joined the army only six months back and is in fact due to attend a year-long training course at the College of Military Engineering in Pune. I tell him to contact me then for follow up therapy.

A last loaded truck slowly makes its way towards us, across the bobbing pontoon bridge and then it is our turn to use it. I wish Arvinder a quick goodbye, get the bike started and am the first to get on the wobbly bridge. It's tricky keeping control of the loaded bike on this structure which has a hump and a dip and a hump and a dip, enough to rattle my bones. Once off it, even the pot-holed road is an improvement. At least it's not moving sideways.

Kishanganj

IF IT WERE not for the frequent milestones and signboards that proclaim it to be a National Highway, NH34 could well be mistaken for the moon. It has potholes that could compete with lunar craters and win. In some places, the road is corrugated. An overloaded truck rocks on the undulating surface but doesn't topple as I overtake it on its right at a slow 10 kmph. This is the worst road I've ever been on and it continues to misbehave until it approaches Farakka where, sighting the Ganges, it abruptly changes character as would a naughty child accosted by a strict parent. It suddenly becomes much nicer and smoother, but only for a while.

Farakka Township, built around the Farakka Barrage and the nearby National Thermal Power Corporation (NTPC) is a different, more disciplined world. Roads and buildings are better maintained. I pass groups of blue uniformed children prancing away to school. After two days of riding through grimness and grime, the sound of their laughter seems doubly precious. The Indian Oil petrol pump I've stopped at is clean and has a coffee shop attached where bike and biker can get their fill.

The Farakka Barrage is one of India's largest and taps the Ganges through a 40 kilometre long feeder canal running south and connecting to the Hoogly. NH34 is taking me across the Ganges, running parallel to the railway tracks. It is a narrow two-way corridor walled on both sides by sheets of steel allowing neither view nor width to overtake. I crawl behind a truck for the entire length of the bridge, breathing diesel.

As soon as the bridge across the Ganges ends, NH34 returns to its old habits but this time with added vigour and vengeance. Many potholes are full of muddy brown water, letting you discover their depth only after delivering a jarring jerk to the base of the spine. It is tough going even for a motorcycle and I can well empathise with the truck and bus drivers who have to ply their big vehicles on this road. Many are stopped by the roadside with broken axels, blown tyres and overheated engines and must provide brisk business for the service stations that dot either side of the road.

I struggle through Malda and suffer through Raiganj taking all that the road can throw at me until deliverance comes at Dalkhola where NH34 ends and I can leave it with a final curse.

I like NH31 from the moment I get on it. Who wouldn't? It is a modern four-lane highway allowing me to finally speed up enough to feel the breeze. NH34 was claustrophobic but now I can breathe again.

There's about 30 minutes of daylight left when I get off the highway and enter Kishanganj (Bihar) where I hope to find a 'good' hotel. I am near the railway station and there are many hotels in this crowded area. One of them is Hotel Puja, a large broad two-storey building with many rooms and a wall shared with the railway station. Ten feet high corrugated steel sheets all around give the place a fortress like look. I ride inside, park and walk three steps up to the reception counter where I have to prove my identity and even show them papers to prove the motorcycle is mine before I am allotted a single room on the first floor for Rs.500.

Raju,(the universal hotel boy who has helped me lug the saddle bags to so many rooms in so many hotels) takes me to a room on the first floor and, like his counterpart in Plassey, tells me I'll have to park the bike inside the garage which is locked up in the night. *'Bahut chori hoti hai'* (Lots of thefts). He also advises me to use my own lock for the door when I go out. Like most other Rajus I've met, this one too is a likeable fellow—not yet twenty but already so worldly-wise and street smart. He looks surprised when I ask him if it is safe for me to go out for dinner. *'Sahab, yahan sab safe hai. Koi tension nahi leneka,'* He says with the nonchalance of an Amitabh Bacchan. Only, I must return before 9 pm because that's when the steel gates are locked.

Just as I begin to ask Raju another question, an amplified voice interrupts with the information that the 15629 Chennai-Guwahati Express, which was to arrive on platform 4 is now expected on Platform 2.

'Railway announcement *hai*,' Raju enlightens me as he unlatches the door to the attached compact balcony. I look out and see that I have an unimpeded view of the platforms of Kishanganj Railway Station. I pull out a 100 rupee note and hand it to Raju who is surprised to get it. Tips are usually given when customers leave. I have learnt to do the opposite ever since I heard Osho deliver a Mullah Naseeruddin joke which went something like this:

> *Mullah Naseeruddin goes to a barber for a haircut and a shave. The barber is not very attentive to him; hurriedly finishes cutting his hair and beard, in the process delivering a few nicks and cuts with his razor. Before leaving, Mullah Naseeruddin gives the barber a gold mohur tip.*
>
> *After a few weeks, Mullah goes to the same barber again. This time he is treated like royalty. The barber is attentive, careful and respectful. There are no bruises on the face this time. Mullah gets up and hands the barber a shrivelled copper coin.*
>
> *'But last time I gave you bad service and still you gave me gold!' exclaims the disappointed hair cutter.*
>
> *Mullah Naseeruddin told him that the copper was for last time's service and the gold mohur was for this one.*

By the time I've taken a cold water wash and changed into cleaner clothes, I have learnt that the Darjeeling Mail is running late by 15 minutes, that coolies have to be paid according to fixed rates and any complaints are to be reported to the station master. Passengers must watch out for pickpockets. Every announcement is followed by a cheery musical message wishing everyone a safe and happy journey.

It is only 6 pm and I decide to escape the audio assault and go explore a town I had never even heard of till today. I walk out onto the street and now, instead of only railway announcements (which I can still hear) my ears have to handle additional inputs from the taxi horns, phut-phutting autorickshaws and other assorted noise makers. I am looking for a restaurant that has mutton *biryani* cooking in its kitchen. I haven't eaten through the day; just thinking about the food is making me salivate like Pavlov's dog. I ask my way to the town's eat-street where I choose Hotel Salman because it looks the busiest. Their *biryani* is still cooking but the *kheema pav* is ready. I go occupy a chair. A plate full of spicy meat mince appears and vanishes. I ask for a repeat order and when that's gone, get up satiated and walk back to Hotel Puja. Raju shows me where I can park the bike. That done I go back to the room and plonk down on the bed. The railway lady is going strong. She tells me not to use the toilets when the train is halted at stations. And then it is time for 15651 Jammu-Tawi Express to arrive and she launches into another tirade of information.

Now hold on...my inner voice reasons with me like a mother would. Passengers do need to know when and where their trains are due. Sometimes one has to just grin and bear it and I prepare myself for a night of disturbed sleep. But I have underestimated the clever mind-body organism that I am. When the system needs rest, it knows how to make the lady's voice recede, making it fade; as if she were walking further and further away...and then...even as she's expressing faint regrets at the inconvenience caused to passengers due to the delay in the arrival of this-or-that train, I can no longer hear her.

In the morning I wake up to loud knocks on the door.

'*Kaun?*' (Who?)

'Raju, sir. *Chai.*'

I must have slept like a log because I've woken up feeling rather chirpy. I unlatch the door and Raju bounces in dressed in *salwaar kameez* and skull cap, and puts a thermos on the table. Yesterday, in his shorts and T-shirt, with a name like Raju, I had assumed he was Hindu. He says he's just returned from *Namaz.*

I begin to sip the tea which looks muddy and tastes watery sweet. Raju sees my frown and says he can get me better tea from the stalls outside. I agree and he takes the flask to return in ten minutes with what turns out to be two cups of strong masala chai, just the way I like it. He's standing around as I begin to collect my belongings and pack the bags. I ask him how long he's been working. Where's he from? Does he have family? Over the next half hour, I come to know that this seventeen-year-old has been working since he was five. His real name is Moinuddin Madari. He has never been to school and can't read or write. He lives with his parents and two sisters in a slum on the railway land nearby. His father had been a *madari* (travelling road side entertainer) as had his grandfather. Once upon a time they were a nomadic family who travelled from village to village performing acrobatics on the roadside. They had a black bear who could dance and a pair of monkeys which had been trained to act out funny husband-wife dramas. But that was all gone now.

I asked him, 'Why? What happened?'

'One day some people came with the police in a van. They said we couldn't keep Bhalubhai or Munna-Munni with us because it was illegal. We were mistreating them. This was not true. Bhalubhai and Munna-Munni were part of our family and we fed them before anyone of us ate.'

With their traditional work taken away, the family had moved to Kishanganj. The father was now a watchman for a wood merchant earning 1500 rupees a month.

I wait for a break in his narration and then ask him about life in Kishanganj. Is it a safe place to live? Are there communal tensions? How's Law and Order? Moinuddin has shed the nonchalance of yesterday's Raju and now appears more real. He says there are 70 per cent Muslims and 30 per cent Hindus here but he has not seen a single riot. *'Kabhi kabhi thoda lafda hota hai. Zyada nahi,'* (There is trouble at times. But not much) he says and walks to the door. Raising a finger upward he says, '*Sab ka malik ek,*' (God is one) and makes his exit in style.

As I load the bike and ride out between the steel-sheet gate of Hotel Puja, I hear her again. She says she regrets any inconvenience caused to passengers but her voice doesn't sound sorry at all.

Elephant, Ahoy!

I AM NOW in a river basin and around me are large tracts of flat farmland, verdant green with a dense cover of young paddy. Collections of thatched houses form small villages all along this road. I've been riding for an hour and feel the need for a break. Stopping by the roadside, I go sit on a milestone to enjoy a bit of immobility. I've attracted the attention of a group of four ten-year-old boys who come and stand grinning around me, saying nothing. I ask them what they want and after a period of more silence, one of them puts his hand out and asks me for a pen which prompts the other three to follow suit and stretch out their hands and make the same unusual appeal. Surprisingly, they don't look at all disappointed when I say I've no pens with me and scamper off emitting peals of laughter as if the joke's on me. Maybe that's the way they get their thrills.

The road continues to cut through farmland which stretches flat around me. This wet, fertile land is recharged every year by rich silt from China. I have a 360-degree-view of green fields fading away into the horizon. It is midday but the fields are empty of any activity. I see no one around. Maybe the planting is done with. I come upon a culvert; a nice place to stop for a private picnic. I finish with my water ritual and go sit on the cement block of a culvert which doubles as a milestone. I can afford to take it real easy today. It's a wonderful day. The green fields, brightly sunlit, are soothing to the eyes which have long focussed on the grey tarmac of the road. Patches of fields are covered with sheets of still water which gleam like mirrors and seem to energise the scene. 100 feet away, a group of egrets takes off and moves to another field.

I feel so much at home here. I must have been a Bengali in my last birth. I just can't stop myself from bursting into song.

O nodi re
ekti kotha shudhai shudhu tomaare
bolo kothae tomar desh
tomar neiki cholaar shesh
O nodi re

So engrossed am I in my reverie that I haven't noticed the approach of two men dressed in the saffron robes of *sadhus*, one with a cow in tow. My song stops in its tracks, leaving me a bit embarrassed. I was in a boat, gliding over the softly rippling waters, singing an ode to the river of life but the sudden presence of these two brings me back to reality.

I smile them a greeting which they respond to in a subdued friendly manner. One smiles and says I sing very well but I didn't sing like a Bengali. Where am I from? Where am I going? I answer their questions and ask a few myself. They are returning from the market in Debra where they have purchased the cow. They are from Jhalia a small village 18 kilometres away.

I ask if they are *sadhus* and they laugh and say no. The reason they're wearing saffron is that it helps them drive a better bargain in big town Debra. 'Traders seek our blessings and give us discounts,' says one. After they leave, I cannot get back to my daydream so get back on the road, amazed at how misleading appearances can sometimes be. First the fake *hijras* of Gurupur, and now these two 'sadhus' from Jhalia. Is no one who he claims to be?

The road has become a bridge flying me over a tributary of the Mahananda and then gliding down into more farm land. A shirtless man walks the road pulling a buffalo, two women sit under a tree on which is nailed a metal plate with a sketch of a bus, an old man fishes in shallow water with a hand-held net. There is natural grace in the faces I glimpse for the three second exposure that a moving bike allows. I notice the women have lustrous hair and then discover the men have them too. Must be all the fish they eat!

The land begins to gently undulate just as I exhaust my stock of the three Bengali songs I know. Two signboards warn of Elephant Crossing but don't make much impact on my mind which is occupied in searching its database for a song to sing next. When a third elephant warning appears, I think wouldn't it be great if I actually see the pachyderms. Thoughts of tigers turn me into yellow jelly (as I proved to myself that Nagzira night), but elephants I can handle. I've seen many on the streets of Pune. They're peaceful creatures. Divine even. I've ridden one (in the Mumbai zoo). So no, I'm not afraid.

The next fifteen minutes would show me how ignorant and arrogant I've been, at least about elephants.

Riding through a sparsely forested section I take no special notice of a car full of people halted by the roadside on the left, but as I pass them, I hear panicked shouts from the car. I stop the bike and look back at the stationary vehicle to find out what the ruckus is about. '*Hathi, Hathi,*' they are yelling from inside the car. I look at the road ahead and see an elephant spraying himself with dry brown mud which he is sucking from the roadside with his agile trunk. He is a magnificent specimen with long matched tusks and is shaking his head from side to side as if refusing to leave. Then he turns his face and sprays one consignment of brown dust in our direction. It is a National Geographic kind of moment and deserves a picture or two. I hear someone shouting again but ignore it, my attention on quickly getting my camera out of the backpack strapped behind me on the rear seat. Oblivious to the danger, I look up, raise my camera and freeze in panic when I see the beast ambling towards me with purpose in its beady eyes. He is not moving in the familiar docile manner of his domesticated cousins. In fact, he looks positively threatening and he's coming on fast.

The camera drops from my hands and clatters on the road (I should have put the strap around my neck as the manual advises). I am glad to have kept the engine running. I quickly turn the bike around and rush back to the waiting vehicles which now include three cars, a truck and an SUV lined one behind the other. A young man shouts at me from the open window of the SUV wanting to know if I'm crazy. The truck driver employs more colourful language. *'Saale, jawani ki masti chadhe hai?'* (Feeling the headiness of youth, are we?) I shout out a loud 'Sorry' and go to the end of the waiting line, thankful to the helmet for hiding my red face. Soon they've forgotten about me. All eyes are on the elephant which has stopped his advance and is now facing sideways. The crowd is chattering. *'Maharaj* is alone today.' 'There might be more following him.'

'Every night they raid our village.'

'I saw many elephants pass by in the night.'

'This is an elephant corridor.'

'He's going.'

'Namaskar, Maharaj.'

'Gone.'

'Wait for 5 minutes.'

I place myself in the middle of the convoy of vehicles as they begin to move. One of the cars stops near my fallen camera and the very man who had asked if I was mad, gets down to pick it up and hands it to me. Everyone is blowing their horns to scare away any animals in the vicinity. As I rush through this human-cum-elephant thoroughfare, I'm no longer singing.

The road becomes safe again as it begins to climb and dip between the large tea estates that are now spread all around me. Imposing houses behind ornate cast iron gates and English names stand amidst low rolling green hills. It's a charming patch of road indeed, like a painting. Tea gardens on the undulating landscape provide a dense, dark green canvas dotted with vivid spots of red, yellow and green—the colour of the *saris* of the women picking tea. They are chanting songs as they fill baskets resting on their backs. I stop and, not unlike a Hindi film hero, wave out to them, expecting them to all wave back as I've seen happen so often on the magic screen. All the reaction I get is a curt warning bark from a chained Doberman who stares at me and growls in a decidedly unwelcoming manner.

NH31 becomes NH31C and continues to take me through more tea estates. I've bypassed Siliguri and now have only a 100 more kilometres to go before the India-Bhutan border.

I get off NH31C at Dalgaon and take a connecting road to Hashimara where SH12A is waiting to take me through some more tea-estates before bringing me to border-town Jaigaon. The evening sun is behind me shining its gold on the ornate pagoda entry gateway. A shadow of me and my bike stretches ahead as if anxious to enter Bhutan before I do.

Entering Bhutan

THIS IS ONE of the few countries where citizens of India are exempt from visa. I will have to register the motorcycle with the Bhutanese Traffic Authority and obtain a no-pollution certificate. All this I've learnt from the all-knowing internet.

The Bhutanese guard manning the entry waves me to a halt and after running his eyes all over me and the bike, asks, 'Indian?' When I nod yes, he nods too and his white-gloved hands gesture me to proceed. No frisking, no asking of any questions, no documents to show. This is the freest border I've ever crossed. In less than the minute it took to change countries, I've entered Phuntsholing which looks quieter, cleaner and more orderly than the chaotic Jaigaon I've just left behind. The roads are broader and some of the buildings have distinct oriental facades with pagoda roofs and intricate wooden trimmings. The population is a mix of Bhutanese shoppers and Indian shop-keepers. Brisk trade is in the air. It is getting dark and lights are being switched on everywhere as I stop to ask a traffic policeman for directions to the GREF Officers' Mess, Project Dantak, where I hope a bed is waiting for me courtesy my good friend Soma who is now a Major General in the Indian Army and has promised to arrange accommodation for me in Thimpu as well. I ride to the Dantak campus, which has a security cabin at the gate, where I show my identity and tell my tale. The guard phones someone who must have confirmed my story because I am issued a pass and directed to a row of twenty cottages one of which is to be mine. I am even assigned a 'Raju'. I convey a million mental thanks to my friend Soma all through the evening. This Raju calls himself Raja but is no different from others when it comes to enthusiastically satisfying each of my requests, be it for laundry service, Old Monk or dinner. I've passed him the standard hundred rupee lubricant of course. Raja even gets me ice. What more could a weary biker ask for? Elephants?

The sun rises prematurely in Bhutan. Bright daylight at 5 am. Too early for even enthusiastic Raja to have tea ready so I put my tea maker to use and with 'everything else'

taken care of, walk out to see my surroundings for the first time. It was dark when I had arrived yesterday. This place doesn't really look like a typical Indian Army Officers' Mess. The ones I've been to before have always had a stiff, clean look about them. This one has the homely personality of low-income housing. Next to it is a 20-foot wide and 15-foot deep concreted trench, half filled with trash which is the Indo-Bhutan border. Across it is noisy India where even as one loudspeaker is summoning Muslims to their morning *namaz*, another is reciting Sanskrit *shlokas* at 150 decibels while a nearby gurdwara competes with an even louder rendering of the *shabad*. Fifty feet away from India, I stand in Bhutan and listen to the casserole of cacophony being exported from across the border.

Today my first priority is to get the entry permit for myself from Bhutan Immigration and a pollution check certificate for the motorcycle from the Bhutan Traffic Authority. This is a small town and the Immigration Office is just off the road nearby. Like most government buildings in Bhutan, this one also has a pleasing oriental elevation with colourful wooden frills and pagoda roofs. A broad corridor on the ground floor leads to a window where I am quickly issued the entry permit. No fee is charged for the document which allows me to travel to Thimpu and Paro. All they need is an ID and two photographs and I've come prepared with both.

The Traffic Authority clearance takes more time. Their offices are a distance away housed in a beautiful white building with a pagoda top, standing in a landscaped garden with large cemented areas reserved for driving tests and pollution checks. Everything looks immaculate. I ride in through the broad gates and park in the designated area, then walk into the building. A young girl in a neat traditional dress actually smiles as she reads my plain-paper application and hands me a form to fill after which I am to take my bike to the testing area. Unlike in India where a visit to the RTO involves dealing with touts and harassed clerks, this RTO is a picture of efficiency, courtesy and honesty. This is where I begin to realize that there is something different about the Bhutanese...a feeling that is to become reinforced in the days that follow.

My bike's emission is satisfactory and I get my clearance certificate without even the suggestion of a bribe. I ride out into a petrol pump, top up the tank and engine oil and decide to explore Phuntsholing, but only from the saddle. I don't feel like walking. The town is one big bazaar crowded with shoppers and looks like any other Indian market except the shopping public is Bhutanese while most shopkeepers are Indian. After riding around a few more streets I get back to the army cottage where Raja is waiting with a bundle of my washed and ironed clothes. Tomorrow on the road, I will look neat and clean.

Dinner arrives in a large hot-case from the army kitchen. I cannot possibly eat it all and leave most of it for Raja to take home. I've been talking with him and know he lives in Jaigaon with his mother and younger sister and commutes across the border every day. He's paid a daily wage of Rs. 100 which he supplements by waiting on periodic guests like me.

I spend the last part of the evening lubricating brain and brawn with the help of a certain elderly gentleman also known as Old Monk before I surrender the day and let the octopussy tendrils of sleep pull me into their fold yet again.

My second morning in Phuntsholing unfolds without a hitch. The electric tea maker makes me tea, the red-glowing light of the water heater promises a hot bath and the toilet flushes emphatically and without hesitation. In short everything works like clockwork and by 10 am, well breakfasted, I have said goodbye to a smiling Raja and let prominent road signs guide me out of town.

Bright sunlight streams in through gaps in low hung dark rain clouds spotlighting patches of the highway to Thimpu. The road has maintained a gentle 20-degree-upward slant ever since I left Phuntsholing an hour ago. Now it has brought me to a vantage point that overlooks the town I've just left. There is a pocket set aside for parking—a good place to stop and take stock.

Immediately below me are the neatly lined buildings of Phuntsholing, separated from each other by broad roads. Larger buildings with beautiful pagoda roofs are everywhere. A flight of grey pigeons is making its rounds over the awakening city.

I raise my head a bit more and am now able to see the plains of India stretching into the southern horizon. A delta of streams runs between green rice fields, spotted with clusters of concrete buildings. From this distance, I can't hear the noise, nor see the crowds. How serene India looks from up here. I look on for some more time before kicking the bike to life. Soon the road turns around a hill and I lose sight of my country.

It's warm enough to ride in just a T-shirt and light cotton trousers. There has been no traffic on the road for the last ten minutes which I find surprising. This is a major road and I'd expected it to be busy. A few more turns around the hills and I come up to the reason—a road block. A huge pile of boulders and mud has crashed onto the road. Two bulldozers are busy clearing it up. I spot a rotund middle-aged Indian man in a brown uniform directing the drivers of the bulldozers. Another bigger machine is half way up the hill scooping out more mud and rock and shoving it downhill to add to the pile below. Many cars and trucks are stuck on both sides of the blockage. This looks like it could be a long wait. I walk to the left of the road which overlooks open fields empty of any habitation, sit on a rock under the shade of a large tree and light a cigarette. A cool breeze is blowing. Brown uniform walks up to me and asks for a cigarette. He offers to pay me for it. I know that sale of tobacco is banned in Bhutan and am carrying a whole carton of 555. I can afford to give him one. It gets him talking. He's a civil engineer with GREF who says the landslide ahead has been caused deliberately. 'We're cutting into the hillside to broaden the road.' The Phuntsholing-Thimpu highway is being revamped into a six-lane expressway and he is in charge of supervising this section.

He's on a three-year posting in Bhutan and enjoying it. 'Beautiful country. Beautiful people,' he says. His family is in Meerut. His children didn't want to leave their school so he had to come alone. We talk some more and then he goes back to work. A gap appears in the mud pile and is just wide enough for a motorcycle to get through.

It is afternoon and beams of strong sunlight shine like laser waves through scattered openings in the dark rain clouds that hang overhead. The road is gold and dark green and the valleys are brimful with mist. The helmet's visor fogs up just like the windshield of a car with closed windows does on a rainy day. It is hazy enough to make me feel I am riding my motorcycle in heaven, through a kingdom shaped by columns of clouds.

But where are the people? I go long distances without spotting any habitation. Finally I see a few shanty shops close to the road. A green sign board on the tin roof of the largest shanty proclaims it to be the Wangdi Lhamo Hotel Cum Bar. It also tells me that I am now in Jumja in district Gedu.

A man of about thirty with the proprietary air of the owner of this establishment, a woman who must be his wife, their son of about five and an elderly woman are all sunning themselves on chairs placed just off the road. I stop in front of their hotel, dismount, greet them and ask if I can get tea here. 'Indian *chai*?' asks the man and when I nod yes, the wife gets up and goes into the shack hotel. The kid runs towards the bike and wants to sit on it. The loaded bike is parked on its side-stand on a slight slope and might well topple on the boy. I get up, wheel the bike onto the flatter tar road and put it up on its main stand. I pick the kid up and put him on the bike seat which pleases the man. He speaks to me in Hindi.

He has a house in Gedu the larger town which is 20 kilometres further up the highway. This is his place of business and the hotel is only one of them. Next to the hotel is a vegetable stall. The auto workshop provides a puncture repair service. And then there is the bar. All these businesses belong to him.

'You manage all these alone?' I ask him.

'My wife, my mother and a helper-boy; we all run this place together.' His father died when he was eighteen. He had been studying for his BSc in Kolkata but had to give that up and return to Gedu. He got government permission to set up this hotel and gradually added his other businesses over the years. As he speaks, he has his eyes on his son who is still sitting on the bike and repeatedly yelling 'brrrrrrrrr' as if he were an Enfield engine.

The lady brings two cups of tea and puts them on the table. She then joins her mother-in-law who has been standing around smiling indulgently at the antics of the boy. This is my first experience of meeting a Bhutanese family. Even though the man tells me his businesses are 'doing well', the family doesn't look rich. I guess I'm conditioned to think of the rich as those who wear designer clothes and drive expensive cars. These four people couldn't be rich. Hotel Wangdi Lhamo is nothing more than a ramshackle structure. From where I am sitting, I get a view of a dingy room with four plastic chairs around a metal table, probably the bar. The vegetable stall has a total of four baskets each holding small quantities of potatoes, cabbages, chillies and beans. The garage looks rusty. As the man talks with me, the women are talking to each other in their own language. Their voices are soft and their actions gentle. The kid has now quietened down and is smiling like an infant Buddha! They do look happy.

The mother and her daughter-in-law suddenly break into laughter over something one of them has said and although I can't understand a word, their glances tell me that they are talking about me. The man has heard it too and responds with a smile.

'My mother thinks you look like Steve McQueen in Great Escape.' I almost respond by saying that she should get her eyes checked but stop myself from what could be interpreted as a rude remark. Instead I ask him what the old lady is chewing. Her reddened lips and tongue, her rotting teeth, her styled and dyed hair, her laughing eyes, her happy demeanour and the maroon gown she's dressed in make her look rather striking. She is drinking a brown liquid which could very well be rum. Maybe that explains why she's in such a jolly mood. There... She's said something funny again which has made even the kid laugh. She covers her mouth with the back of her left hand every time she lets out a cackle.

'She chews *doma*. It is like your Indian *paan*,' the man replies to the question I had almost forgotten I'd asked. He then fishes out a silver box from his pocket and opens it to reveal his own stock of *doma*. Green leaf wrapped around some stuffing. He picks one out and extends it in my direction. Sure it looks like an Indian *paan* but when I put it in my mouth and begin to chew, I know I've made a mistake. Unlike its sweet, aromatic Indian counterpart, *doma* has an unpleasant stink to it. Then my mouth begins to burn. I walk a distance away and spit my mouth's contents out into the mud. When I return I see the man is laughing as are the women. Obviously I have failed the test. He says *doma* is part of Bhutanese tradition—sanctified by the gods to keep them warm. I believe it. It is making me sweat. I rinse my mouth and finish drinking the tea for which I pay the man 10 rupees. (Indian currency is accepted all over Bhutan at par with their own Ngultrum). I am ready to go but the kid is still in his bike-rider avatar and refuses to relinquish his seat. When I try to pull him off, he lets out a loud angry howl in protest. I let go of him and look at the father who nods his head and gets off the chair. The kid lets out a fresh bawl and tightens his grip on the handle when he sees his father approach him. I expect the man to get angry and forcibly pull the kid off the bike. Instead, standing next to his son, he begins an impromptu mime act. He extends his arms as if gripping an imaginary bike. Brrrrr Brrrrrrr Brrrrr he yells and goes around the kid a few times simulating a bike ride. The boy's crying has lost its vehemence but he continues to whimper for a while. Then he stretches his arms towards his father who picks him off the bike and says something in Bhutanese. The kid runs away looking appeased and happy. 'I told him to go and draw a picture of the kind of motorcycle he would like to ride. He likes to draw.'

Happy to have regained possession of my bike, I wish him goodbye and leave before the kid changes his mind.

A Paradise Called Gedu

THE ROAD TO Thimpu continues to snake around the densest of forests lining deep valleys and steep hillsides. Another hour of this and sporadic habitations begin to dot either side of the highway which now broadens as it enters the small township of Gedu. On my right, there are a few apartment buildings lined up parallel to the highway. Further down, I can see small farms with wooden houses scattered on the descending slopes of the valley. It strikes me that the whole place looks absolutely deserted. It is 4 pm but there is no one around for me to ask about hotels and such. I've decided to break journey here.

On my left, leading up a slight incline are three large buildings painted bright white, which are now glowing in the evening sun. Although they look like offices or maybe hostels, each building is crowned with ornate red pagodas giving them a palace-like look. They stand apart, amidst well kept gardens. Flowers of various colours bloom all around. I ride up to the nearest building, park my loaded bike in a designated area and walk up the twenty-foot wide entry steps into a rather narrow passageway, a corner of which has been made into a reception counter. A wooden board on the wall says TALA Hydro-Electric Project, Officers' Hostel.

So I've chanced on a hostel! Let's hope I can talk myself into a room here. The only problem? There is no one to ask. I walk out and go sit on a bench in the garden to wait in the hope of meeting a live human amidst this fairy land. Right now I only have the occasional rustle of the breeze for company. There is still a lingering raw tingle in my mouth, thanks to the *doma*.

Gedu remains pin-drop quiet. Where are all the people? Ah! There is one, walking up the incline towards me. I get off my perch to go meet him half way. He is dressed in a striking manner. A yellow checked, traditional Bhutanese gown ending just below the knees. Long black knee high socks instead of pants, shiny brown shoes and a jungle-camouflage De Gaul cap which adds two inches to his 5'5" frame. He has a military manner and I'm not surprised when he tells me he's security. Who am I? He's talking in Hindi. As I tell him my story, he brings out a silver box from a pocket and supplies himself a *doma*. His mouth, teeth and lips get a new coat of dark red. After I finish my story, he says he's very happy to meet me. He formally introduces himself as Commander Phurpha and shakes my hand. I can stay in the hostel but since I am not a bonafide official or engineer, I would need to get special permission from his boss. We then walk back into the reception area where he calls up his superior on the internal landline, explains the matter and then hands me the phone, saying the boss wants to talk to me. The voice at the other end turns out to be a Mr Iyer, originally from Chennai. I repeat my story and Mr Iyer says ok and wants to talk to Phurpha again. My benefactor listens, hangs up the phone, then leads me up a broad staircase to the third floor and unlocks corner room no. 302 at the end of a long corridor. It is a small, single room with a tiny balcony which offers me a panoramic view of a darkening sky over a fairy tale Gedu, twinkling with lights. I can also see my bike standing alone in the lighted parking below.

Commander Phurpa is quite a talkative fellow. He tells me that the campus I'm on is currently being used by the Engineers of the TALA Project but will become the Royal Bhutan University once the Hydro Electric Project is operational next year. I am quite hungry and ask him if the hostel has a canteen. Yes, he says. Dinner is between 7 and 8 pm. And since everyone using the hostel is Indian, I can expect Indian food. He adds that the TALA project is designed, financed and executed by India which will then buy the extra hydro-electricity generated. I bring his attention back to food. I tell Phurpha that I can get Indian food in India. Here, I want to eat what the locals eat. Aren't there any Bhutanese restaurants in Gedu? This appears to please him. He nods and says he can take me to a local eatery. But he has to first visit the *gompa* for his evening prayers and I am welcome to accompany him. The local *gompa* is a three kilometre walk back along the highway and it is already dark by the time we get there. We enter the *gompa* through a broad ceremonial gate which leads us into a courtyard alight with flickering candles. Young boys with shaven heads, dressed in maroon robes are prancing about the cobbled stone floor. A young couple sits chatting on a stone bench in one corner. Along the corridor, the revolving prayer drums are in constant motion, spurred on by the stream of devotees, most dressed in traditional garments. There are some very old people walking about whirling their own miniature prayer drums.

Phurpha is a popular figure here. He is greeted enthusiastically by many people in the *gompa*. Bhutanese people talk ever so softly with each other and their speech is punctuated by sounds of gentle mirth. Phurpha leads me to the main temple which has an ornate ten-foot brass statue of a sitting Buddha. I stand in front of the Buddha, fold my hands, close my eyes and pretend to pray. When I open them, I notice Phurpa standing near the door talking to two young sarong-clad women, all three of them looking in my direction. As I join them, Phurpa tells me that the two girls are sisters and have a patient for me to see. 'Patient?' I ask surprised. He says that the girls' mother has lost her speech and since I am a speech doctor, could I examine her? They live just nearby.

I am tired after a rather long day in the saddle and hungry to boot. But I couldn't very well refuse, so I say, 'Sure,' with as much enthusiasm as I can muster.

We walk back to town on the well-lit road and come upon a collection of small houses standing close to each other. The dwellings have low tin roofs and I am led into a small windowless room lit yellow by a low watt bulb. The place is stuffed with furniture inch to inch. Posters and framed family photos crowd the low walls.

My patient is a frail woman sitting on a bench in a corner watching muted TV. The daughters give me the case history. Mother has stopped talking. Until six months ago, she used to talk with everyone. But now she doesn't say a word.

I ask questions and find out that she had been widowed early. Their father had died in an accident when she and her sister were very young. She's been a very good mother to them and still works hard. But she doesn't say a word.

I go and sit next to the lady who has been watching me. She smiles and nods and moves to make space for me on her narrow bench. The daughters say she understands everything and does all her normal housework. Why is she not talking? They had taken her to doctors in the General Hospital in Thimpu who couldn't do anything for her. She's even gone to a well known *shaman* who said the spirits were angry with their family and had struck their mother dumb. They had prescribed a ritual which included sacrificing a white rooster. It hadn't helped.

I take the lady's hand and squeeze it. She squeezes back with a firm grip. I ask her to move her tongue left to right and up and down, which she can. I ask her to cough but try as she might, she's not able to produce even the faintest of coughing sounds. Either both her vocal cords are paralysed (an extremely rare condition) or she's lost her will to speak. This lady needs a complete neurological and psychiatric evaluation, not a cursory one by a tired and hungry speech therapist. But I had to do my bit. I go through the motions of demonstrating some breathing and voice exercises she could do, knowing she wouldn't. When I get up to go, one of the girls places a full bottle of whiskey in my hand. 'Consultation fee,' she says. Having done nothing to deserve it, I tell her I cannot accept her gift but Phurpha thinks otherwise. He smiles and deftly takes the bottle from my hands and puts it away in one of the pockets of his chequered attire. He then leads me into the local restaurant bar which is a tiny tin shack of a place with shaky narrow wooden benches along two walls around a rickety table. A naked light bulb hangs from the ceiling.

A man is sitting alone on one of the benches with his head drooping down as if he were dozing. On the table in front of him is a glass half full of whiskey. We go and occupy the other bench and in the process make enough noise to wake him up. Apparently the man is not as drunk as our first impression of him might have suggested. He looks up and smiles sadly at Phurpha who introduces him to me as Pema Tobgi, an engineer who works in Arikha province.

Phurpha pulls out my consultation fee and yells, '*Pani!*' in answer to which a woman in her thirties brings a plastic jug of water and three glasses. She puts them on the table and sits next to him. He pours whiskey for the three of us and talks to the woman in a language I can't follow.

She finishes her drink rather quickly, says something to the two men and gets up to go. Phurpa tells me she's gone to cook our meal. 'Nice lady,' he says, licks his lips and downs his drink. He turns to Pema and asks when he is getting married in English. Then, turning to me he laughs and says, 'This guy is twenty-eight years old,' as if that explains everything. I think my commander friend is drunk. The bottle of whiskey is more than half gone and I've only had one peg. He is needling the engineer into reacting but Pema doesn't oblige him. Instead, he calmly tells Phurpha that he will never marry. He doesn't like women at all. They are still talking in English for my benefit which makes me suspect they are playing out a joke, just for fun. I get into the act and ask Pema why and he says he doesn't know why but he has never had any interest in sex and doesn't like to talk to women. Phurpha asks him if he's gay. No, he's not, Pema replies. 'Nag…nag…nag…women nag all the time,' he says, 'and now you are nagging me too.' He gets up and leaves abruptly without a word to anyone of us. So it wasn't a joke after all. That guy was seriously upset. Phurpha looks at me and circles his index finger by the side of his head in the universal sign for loony. He pours more whiskey for both of us. I offer him a cigarette which he appears delighted to smoke. Just to make him think sober, I ask him about tobacco and liquor laws in Bhutan. No one can sell tobacco, but alcohol? 'No problem finding booze here. Very popular!' he says and takes another swig from his busy glass.

The nice lady comes in and clears away part of the crowded table. She returns with two steaming bowls on a tray. One is heaped full with brown fat grained rice while the other has chunks of pork in a watery sea of radish and whole red chillies. It looks and smells so non-appetising that hungry as I am, I can't push myself to eat it. Instead I sip my drink. When Phurpa asks me why I'm not eating, I tell him I am vegetarian. I pay the lady the fifty rupees she's asked for and Phurpa and I walk back to the TALA campus. I can see no one else on the road although it is only 9 pm. Phurpha hasn't let go of my consultation fee which he is now tipping straight into his mouth. He is talking and laughing loudly enough for the entire town to hear him. By the time we've reached the hostel, he's finished with the bottle. He then swaggers unsteadily towards a garbage bin and deposits the empty bottle in it. 'Cannot take bottle home,' he says and stumbles away into the night on the silent, well lit road.

I go up to my room, eat a fistful of cashews and one full *laddoo* to keep stomach acids at bay. When sleep finally comes, it is spiced with a saucy dream in which Pema has eloped with the voiceless woman deeming her his ideal wife—someone who can never nag him!

It's morning and time to drop all the madness of last night and first go feed myself in the now-open canteen on the first floor. Ah...real food! Two *idlis* followed by a huge *dosa* and topped by two glasses of filter coffee. Now I feel normal again. I pack my bags and drag them down to the bike. No Raju here!

The TALA campus has been beautifully designed with many white painted buildings of various sizes scattered amidst landscaped gardens shaded with young trees. Even the larger buildings are made to look artistic and quaint with their typical Bhutanese elevation.

A large mural at the gate has colourful assorted depictions of mountains and swirling white clouds and dragons, of course. By its side is the security cabin. The immaculately dressed guards are polite and wish me a happy journey. Nobody seems to abuse their authority here.

As I ride out of Gedu, a tingle of happiness is running through me.

Thimpu

THE PHUNTSHOLING-GEDU-THIMPU HIGHWAY continues to cut through spectacular scenery. Waterfalls cascade down densely forested slopes, fluffy white clouds hang suspended over the valleys, a benign sun peeps through trees as I turn and twist and turn and twist... The road goes up and down swinging left and right and demands focused riding. An hour of it before I come to the much written about Dantak Canteen which stands perched on a flat rocky outcrop and overlooks another deep valley. Built essentially for GREF staff, the canteen also caters to travellers on the Phuntsholing-Thimpu highway and offers Indian food.

Twelve shining black Royal Enfield motorcycles are lined up on the concrete parking lot, each with a helmet placed over the right rear-view mirror. I add mine to the row and walk into the dining hall expecting to see it full of bikers. Full the hall certainly is with not a table to spare. Around twenty white foreigners (men and women), are sitting in groups around tables—eating, talking and laughing. From their language and accents, they sound American. They all look recently retired—not one of them must be under sixty. Black or tan leather jackets and colourful headscarves bustle about the hall carting plates of food from the self-service counter.

I get my own sandwich and tea and, there being no available sitting place inside, walk out to the parapet overlooking the valley where, propelled by gently blowing breeze, a titanic-shaped white cloud is passing within touching distance.

Two of the American bikers are out admiring the view. I walk over to them and say, 'Hi'. Americans are easy people to talk to. They tell me they're all members of a Harley riders' club from Napa Valley, California. They've been riding in Bhutan through last week and are now on their way back to their starting point—Baghdogra where they will return their rented bikes and fly back home. Their tour has been arranged by an agency in New Delhi which has transported the brand new 500 cc bikes to Baghdogra for them. They have a bus accompanying them carrying their luggage, a mechanic and a cook. We share some more of this and that after which we say our goodbyes and I get back on the road.

When it is completed in 2009 this road will be silky smooth but today, this part of it is an obstacle course of mud, grit, loose stones and potholes. Diversions abound. But I don't have too far to go now. 35 kilometres separate me from the GREF campus in Simtokha which is to be my halt for the next two nights.

Soon I come to the Chuka Check Post where my entry permit will be checked. This is again a simple procedure. I extend my permit through a square opening at the bottom of the netted window. Unseen hands take it. A rustle of a register and a slam of a rubber stamp later, the hands return me the permit—all in less than 5 minutes.

When I return to my bike I see it is surrounded by a group of men in the blue uniform of Bhutan police. They smile at me as I approach and I greet them and shake hands with each of the seven. They are not carrying guns. Not even batons. Three of them are very young, probably new recruits. The others are more senior and talk to me in broken Hindi. There is not even a hint of condescension or discourtesy in their manner. They seem happy to chit-chat. When I offer them cigarettes, every one of them takes one and smokes it with obvious relish. The guilty pleasure of forbidden fruit! Tea appears followed by a second round of smoking this time only by the seniors. At the rate my stock of cigarettes is disappearing, it seems I should have packed two cartons.

An hour out of Chuka, the well marked road indicates the right turn to Simtokha where the GREF campus stands in the crotch between two roads. This time I am housed in a bungalow which overlooks a basketball field. The house has space enough for three families and their uncles but I am the only occupant today. I select my bedroom from the three that the attendant shows me. He's a serious looking fellow, around thirty years of age. He gives single-word answers to my questions so all I discover is that he is from Kolkata and upset not to be home for the ongoing Durga puja. *'Chutti nahi diya,'* (Didn't give me leave) he says grumpily as if blaming me for it. He asks if I want tea.

I look out and see that the sun has set. I tell him to get me some water instead.

And ice if they have it.

Thimpu is only 8 kilometres from Simtokha. The capital city of Bhutan is located in a broad valley and lined with low green hills all around. A river runs by the expressway which descends into the city from a height providing a bird's eye view of the capital. There are no sky scrapers here. Two or three storey buildings, most sporting the pagoda design with extensive frills of carved polished woodwork, house various shops and government departments, most painted white. I park next to other two-wheelers in a designated area on Main Street. I leave my helmet unsecured on the seat and walk away, somehow confident that no one will touch it. On my right is an archery ground where groups of men, all dressed traditionally are practising the national sport. The ground is a large expanse allowing for long range archery. I estimate the bull's eye to be at least 400 meters away. A long shot! A group of four now begin to perform a ritual dance with their bows in hand and quivers strapped on their backs. I stop and take some pictures.

Thimpu conducts its business in a relaxed, leisurely manner. It's 10 am and the street is crowded with office goers, shoppers and many school children who are all dressed in beautiful colour-coordinated uniforms. Groups of young boys and girls move about punctuating their easy chatter with peals of laughter.

No horns honk on the central street of Thimpu and traffic seems to move smoothly without a single traffic light. Only one crossing has a traffic island where a policeman in a crisp blue uniform and wearing white gloves directs the flow of traffic with the grace of a music composer conducting his orchestra.

I've been walking the pavements for two hours now, peeping into shops, looking for gifts for friends and family but they offer me 'Made in China' stuff which I could probably buy back home.

I pass a cinema hall which is reminiscent of pre-multiplex days. A large cloth poster which looks hand-painted depicts a collage of scenes from *Khadrel* a recently released local film. Although the grilled steel gate of the theatre is open, there is no one around. The strong stink of *doma* pervades the air inside and makes me drop any thoughts of going into the theatre to see a Bhutanese movie. There's a restaurant near where I've parked my bike and I enter it more to rest my legs than to lunch. It is a small place with three chequered-cloth covered tables. Seated at one is a monk dressed in Buddhist colours, sipping coffee. I go occupy the next table and sit facing him. He is smiling so I smile back. It strikes me how perfectly round his face is, like the moon. A young boy comes out from the kitchen and takes my order of sandwiches and coffee. The monk sends me another beaming smile which emboldens me to say 'Hello' to which he replies with a '*Namaste.*' He gestures for me to come and sit at his table.

Rinchen Dorji is a travelling monk currently visiting a monastery in Paro. He travels all over Bhutan and other countries like Laos, Cambodia, Vietnam, Thailand and Sri Lanka. He's been to India many times. Some places he is a student and other places he is a teacher.

I ask him what he teaches.

'How to master feelings.'

'You mean like controlling anger?'

'Not controlling. Mastering. Controlling involves suppression. A master suppresses nothing. A master can choose how he wants to feel. Feelings become his slaves instead of vice versa.'

'Can we really do that?'

'Sure,' he says, 'how would you like to feel right now?'

There is something very attractive about this man. Is it

his soft voice? Or the bemused expression on his face? He looks so clean and radiant.

My food arrives and we lapse into silence as I chomp through the sandwiches. After I've finished eating and drinking, he asks me what I'm doing in Thimpu. I point to the parked bike visible through the window and tell him I've come to Bhutan to check out their GNH theory. The monk looks at me with renewed interest. 'So have you found the secret formula for happiness?' he asks me. Like most people here, he too constantly ends each sentence with a laugh. He's laughing now. Before I can think of a smart answer, he's got up. He tells me he's been waiting for a friend who is to drive him back to Paro and he has to leave now.

'Can I meet you in Paro?' I ask him. I've already planned to ride there tomorrow. I want to hear more about mastering emotions. Wouldn't that be great? To be able to choose how we want to feel and for however long! Maybe Rinchen Dorji could tell me how.

But he will be busy with students earlier in the day. We can meet for lunch. He hands me a card with a number to call. We pay our individual bills and walk out of the restaurant.

I have one more task to perform before I head back to Simtokha. Find a hotel in Thimpu. My army accommodation, comfortable though it is, is isolating me from everything Bhutanese. I might as well be sitting in my own home. As they say, I need to get out of my comfort zone.

A stretch of boutiques selling designer clothes, handbags and watches lines a part of the road I am walking on. Attached to one end is a tall building calling itself Centre Mall. In addition to shops and restaurants, it also houses Centre Lodge where I hope to get a room. This is the heart of downtown Thimpu. A signboard directs all those seeking accommodation in Centre Lodge to one of the restaurants 'The Rice Bowl' on the first floor. The restaurant is buzzing with customers. The decor is Chinese so could the food be otherwise? Two neatly groomed young girls dressed in aprons matching the red chequered table covers are busy carting steaming plates from the kitchen. The lady at the counter is hand-writing a bill and once she's added it up, puts it between leather flaps and places it on a plate then adds four Chinese fortune cookies which she has fished out from a jar under the counter. She must have been a beautiful woman in her younger days. She's made it to fifty with much of her charm intact. She's wearing a golden gown which along with her gold-dyed hair makes her stand out against the predominantly red and white decor of the restaurant. When I tell her I'm looking for a room her face takes on an expression of extreme regret. Pouting her thin lips she says all rooms are full. She's very, very sorry but 'No vacancy today.' I say I actually want the room for tomorrow and again her expression changes, this time to portray extreme delight. 'No problem for tomorrow. Very welcome tomorrow.' Then a shadow of doubt plays on her face. 'But you can have it only after 5 pm. Ok?' The current occupants will vacate it at 4. That fits in perfectly with my plans. I can ride back here from Paro, collecting my luggage from Simtokha on the way. My agreement to arrive only after 5 pm tomorrow brings the beatific smile back on the lady's face. She happily accepts the advance and merrily writes out the receipt which she then puts on a tray, adding a fortune cookie before extending it towards me. I slip the cookie into my pocket and leave.

I ride back to Simtokha, and spend the rest of my last evening watching the first India-Pakistan ODI cricket match being played in Guwahati with Mr Grumpy in attendance. He remains monosyllabic throughout the match, successfully curtailing his excitement even when Tendulkar snaps up two quick Pakistani wickets to the relief of an entire nation. But he cannot contain himself when Dhoni hits the winning runs. As the crowds on TV go ballistic, Mr No-Longer-Grumpy and I are both shaking hands and brimming with the joy Indians feel when their team beats Pakistan! I hand him a 100-rupee reward which he accepts as if he himself was man of the match.

Back in my room, changing, the fortune cookie I got from the golden lady falls out of my upended trousers. I pick it up, take it into the bathroom and crush it open over the toilet. The white strip of paper inside has advice for me. 'Treat Your Shadow With Respect.' I wonder how I'm to do that. There must be a deeper meaning to it. Maybe it means treat yourself with respect? But then why not say so straight? Why involve the shadow? And what does one do at night when there is no shadow? Like right now on this darkened bed, I have no one, not even my shadow for company. There's a quick way to remedy the situation. I switch on the side lamp and find my shadow sleeping next to me. Following cookie's instructions to the T, I turn to my shadow and wish it good night in a voice dripping with respect. I have to wipe the dribble off my lips but that done, I switch the lights off and let the shadow sleep.

My last thought is a vague suspicion that I might be losing it.

Paro

BHUTAN IS A biker's paradise and the road I'm on today is picture postcard perfect. Rough in patches but running through a wide river basin which allows for longer stretches of flatter surface.

The green mountains have become brown hills and the valleys now have space enough for some large buildings. The road climbs and curves keeping company with the river which flows at the bottom of the valley to my right. Scattered habitations of beautiful houses and farms dot the landscape. But again, there are very few people around. The only ones I encounter on the road are labourers from India working on road maintenance. Steel bridges span tributaries of River Paro. I stop on one. Once the engine is switched off, it takes about a minute for my ears to become sensitive enough to hear the gurgle of water as it flows below me. I lean on the railings, close my eyes to the dazzling sunlight and listen to the river. The waters are singing a frisky melody. Yesterday, they were immobile glacier. Today they are free to frolic. Five minutes of this audio-meditation soothes mind and body. But now I have a problem. Must be all that water I've been listening to because now I have to pee and I don't know what the rule-book here says about doing it in the open. I haven't seen anyone in Bhutan pissing by the roadside and don't want to embarrass myself in a foreign country. What will they think of India? But try as I might, the call of the bladder cannot be ignored. Biology wins over national pride and allows me just enough time to go down the side of the road and get into position. A concluding shiver of pleasure and I'm done. All through this exercise, I've been avoiding eye-contact with the road in case a car is driving by. But now, with my zip up, I feel confident enough to raise my head and look around. I see no one except a pair of yellow birds who, after a minute of debate between themselves, twitter me their promise not to tell.

The road continues on a gentle incline till it brings me to a point where I get a view of the Paro Airport; its single runway gleaming at the bottom of the valley on my right. This is the country's only airport and only the national carrier Druk is authorised to use it. The approach and take off are reportedly tricky and looking at the terrain around, I can well believe it.

Another half hour's ride on a descending road and I am

on the outskirts of Paro which is spread out before me under a now cloudy sky. I stop by a field where farm hands are tying up brown corn and loading it up in a cart. Rain clouds seem to rest on the higher mountains in the far distance. Scattered on the hills to my right are houses of various sizes. From single room dwellings to large palatial buildings, all seem to have a picture-book neatness about them. Higher up on the cliffs are monasteries with fluttering flags on slanting poles sticking out of their walls. They seem to have been designed to test the resolve of anyone who wants to reach their sanctified domain. I do hope Rinchen doesn't live in one of these cliff hangers. I call the number on the card he's given me and am told that Rinchen Dorji has left a message for me. We are to meet inside Shop No. 74 on Main Street at noon.

Broad tarred roads lead me on to Main Street lined with square blocks of buildings, all looking like each other. Each is identical—three storeys in height, painted in light pastel shades with the typical ornate wooden windows and doors which are a trademark of Bhutanese architecture. Brightly coloured frescos of dragons, deer and flowers are tattooed on the walls and columns of the walking arcade. There are only a few people around, and they are walking around as if they had all the time in the world. No one is rushing about in business suits and briefcases here. No advertising, no neon lights, no policemen, no designer shops and no beggars.

Five minutes before the clock strikes the hour, I walk

into the Meena Restaurant and Bar which is what shop number 74 is. Rinchen Dorji is sitting at a corner table with two other older monks. They all half get up and greet me with handshakes and smiles and then settle back in their chairs. Rinchen Dorji performs the introductions. The other two men have come to Paro from their *dzong* in northwestern Bhutan to attend his course. Turning to them he speaks in Bhutanese. When he's finished, both the older guys look at me and nod their heads and smile but don't say a word.

'They cannot speak English,' Rinchen Dorji explains. 'Only Dzongkha.'

Despite its ornate exterior, the interior of Meena Restaurant and Bar is quite ordinary. Cane chairs around laminate-topped tables. The menu is chalked up on a board near the entry. Curry rice or chicken momos are the choices on offer today. We opt for both and wait for the food to arrive.

'So how do you like Bhutan?' Rinchen Dorji asks me and then laboriously translates everything I say into Dzongkha for the other two who continue to nod and smile at me. I tell them how much and why I'm impressed with what I've seen of their country. I tell them the reasons that brought me here. I make a brief mention of my work in Pune and of Rahul. Lunch arrives and offers an opportunity to switch the conversation from me to them.

'Sir,' I ask Dorji with an intentional touch of formality. 'What you said yesterday, about mastering feelings. Can you say something more?'

He breaks into hearty laughter as do the other two when he tells them what I've said. Then, turning to me, he says, 'We have a body and we have a mind. The body is material and easier to handle. Basic care is all it requires. However, when it comes to our minds—our thoughts and feelings—we are not in the driver's seat.

For example, we don't know what we will be feeling in the next ten minutes. Anything can happen which can make us either happy or angry or sad or afraid, etc. Most people are at the mercy of their feelings which take them on a roller coaster ride of emotions. Wouldn't it be good if we could rule our emotions rather than be ruled by them?'

The other two obviously don't understand a word that he is saying but such is their faith in their teacher that they nod their approval anyway. Rinchen Dorji looking at his watch, says something to them and the two get up, shake my hand and leave.

'I told them to go back to the *dzong* and tell the other students that I will be late. I must complete what I'm telling you. Let us walk.'

He doesn't let me pay, telling me with a wink that his monastery pays for everything. I pick up my backpack and follow him out. My motorcycle is parked right in front of the restaurant and he says I can leave my backpack on it. No need to carry it. I take a quick mental inventory, decide there is nothing in the bag that I cannot afford to lose and follow his advice. As we walk side by side on the road, he is silent for a while, as if collecting his thoughts.

Then he says, 'Purposefully feeling the way I want to feel... We are practising this—Purposeful Feeling. We choose how we want to feel for five minutes. There are meditations to feel happy or angry or sad or even miserable.'

'But why would anyone want to feel sad or miserable on purpose?'

'One can never know the opposite unless one knows *the opposite*. Our senses react in known ways to how we are feeling at that moment. When we are happy, our body feels different from when we are unhappy. Right?'

I nod like I've seen the other two do.

'We begin our meditations by first observing our bodily functions objectively, without trying to alter them.'

'Like Vipassana?' I put in my two-bits.

'Exactly like Vipassana at first. But later we move ahead and meditate on the various sensations that our feelings arouse. How does my body feel when my mind is feeling happy...or angry...? That information is filed away in our memory. Later when I decide I want to feel happy all I have to do is to retrieve that file and replicate that feeling.'

'We also meditate on playing with various feelings— because all feelings are fun to experience if we become their masters and they our slaves. If we don't go overboard when we are happy, our sadnesses also don't seem so sad. We learn how to be not-serious about emotions. Only then can one play with them and enjoy them.'

I wish we were sitting down so I could focus better on

what he is saying. He's walking at a brisk pace which makes it difficult for me to give his talk the attention it deserves. Right now I feel more confused than enlightened.

We have come away from the shopping area and turn into a side street. 'That's my *dzong*,' he says pointing to a gate surrounded on all sides by a fence of green shrubbery. 'I wish we had more time,' he extends both his hands to enfold mine in a *Namaste*-cum-handshake. He walks to the gate and pushes the brass studded black wood door. Bells tinkle and he has disappeared before I can even thank him for the lunch.

Feeling like a kite left adrift, I walk to my bike and ride back to Simtokha.

When I reach the guest house, the man of yesterday's match is waiting for me. He looks a lot more relaxed now and cannot be called Mr Grumpy anymore. I ask him why he is looking so happy and what his name is.

He is Deven Majumdar and he's happy because his leave has finally been sanctioned. He's leaving for Kolkata tomorrow. He'll be meeting his family after six full months, he says as he brings my bags down the steps to my waiting bike.

'*Kal raat ka match mein maza aaya*,' (Yesterday night's match was fun) says the changed man and salutes me a good bye. I wish him a happy holiday and ride out of the GREF campus to take the right turn on the road to Thimpu.

At the Centre Lodge, I am spared an encounter with the VHL (Very Happy Lady) and shown my room by a thin small statured Nepali woman who brings in clean towels and replaces the sheets on the twin beds. Maybe I am imagining it but I sense her eyes weighing me up. She says room service can bring me dinner from The Rice Bowl downstairs and she can supply any liquor I might want. Do I like whiskey?

I wonder if she's part of a gang which plans to get me drunk and then either rob me or accuse me of rape or both. Or then, maybe I've been watching too much crime TV? I tell her I don't drink whiskey emphasising the last word to save myself from the sin of lying. After she leaves, I throw off my clothes, and stay under the shower, soaping and washing myself until I feel clean enough to use the white towels of Centre Lodge. I further pamper my refreshed body with rum and Chicken Manchurian from the restaurant downstairs. The fortune cookie which has come with the dinner has new advice for me,

'Do not mistake temptation for opportunity.'

I spend away the evening watching Bhutan TV until I succumb to the tempting calls from the Sirens of Sleep.

I'm on Bhutan TV

IT IS 10 am of my second day in Centre Lodge. I've pulled down the blinds to shade out the sun and am sipping my third cup of black tea courtesy my loyal tea maker. I've talked myself out of the initial plan to do touristy things today. I've spent half of yesterday doing just that. I'm done with trudging up monasteries and whirling prayer wheels. I've visited the newly built National Memorial, the Taschichho Dzong by the banks of the Wangchhu River, the Textile Museum and the Handmade Paper Factory. Yesterday, I walked and walked and walked. Today, I want to do something useful. Watching news on the National TV network, I have had some difficulty understanding their English. The newsreaders were not talking clearly. A few simple corrective techniques could help them become better speakers. Maybe my professional skills could help? I decide to visit them and offer my services. Let's see how it goes.

Bath and breakfast later, I walk to Main Street, flag down a white Maruti taxi and ask the boyish driver if he'll take me to the Offices of the Bhutan Broadcasting Service (BBS).

When I try to get in through the rear door, he gestures for me to take the front passenger seat instead. The rear seat is already occupied by another youngster who the driver says is his friend.

'Hope you don't mind.'

I shrug and say it's fine with me. A minute passes but we're still stationary. I look at the driver who smiles at me rather charmingly, and again says, 'Hope you don't mind,' this time pointing to the back seat. I turn and see that the 'friend' is busy burning a chunk of something dark green which begins to emit acrid-sweet smoke. Guy is rolling a joint of hashish. Deftly he rolls the hash and tobacco-mix into a joint and passes it to the driver who lights it and inhales deeply. He does it twice and passes the joint back to the friend. The duo continues to smoke the joint until it is too tiny to hold. With its windows closed, the car is full of hash smoke and I'm breathing it. I want to roll the window down but the lever is missing. My effort gets me one more, 'Hope you don't mind,' from the driver.

Nothing happens for the next minute.

I've been expecting to hear the driver start the car but he's just looking at me with glazed eyes and smiling as if he is in a happier world. Now the passenger in the back starts singing. The grinning driver turns his torso in my direction and begins to thump the back of my seat with a basic beat, making my body move in rhythm. Soon the light-weight taxi is shaking to the beat of a local song. I'm surprised to see hash being smoked right on the main street of the capital. Bhutan discourages even tobacco. Not wanting to find out what would happen if the police took an interest in this merry duo, I click open the door and as I get out, I hear the driver say, 'Sorry... Very Sorry... Hope you don't mind.'

I hail another cab, this time driven by a more sober, elderly gentleman. It turns out to be a ten minute drive up an incline culminating at a security gate with a uniformed guard. I feel a buzz in my head and, momentarily disoriented, almost trip on tangled feet as I come out of the cab. The guard must think I am drunk. When he asks me who I want to meet, I don't know what to say. My body language transmits my self-doubt to the guard who now wants to know if I have an appointment with anyone inside. When I tell him I'll talk with anyone, he says to come tomorrow. Everyone is quite busy today. I thank him and begin to walk away thinking it was just a shot-in-the-dark idea anyway, when a loud, 'Hello... Hello,' makes me turn around. A man is waving to me from an open, first-floor window of the building, gesturing me to wait. Soon the man who is in national dress appears at the gate.

'Hello. How can I help you?' he asks pleasantly.

When I tell him about myself, he laughs and exclaims, 'I knew there was a story in you when I spotted you from my window!'

He introduces himself as Tshewang Dendrup. He doesn't say it but from the way the watchman has saluted him, I presume he must be someone important at the BBS. He looks just about thirty-five years old and has an air of bouncy happiness around him. He instructs the security man to make out a pass for me.

'Come please, we will go to my office.' I am guided into the building, up the first floor and into a small room with a table with books and papers spread around the glowing screen of a desktop. Hastily clearing up his desk, he asks me to sit and then leaves the room to return with two mugs of coffee.

He has many questions for me which I am glad to answer. Turns out he is a Royal Enfield fan and an India fan too. Like many Bhutanese, he speaks good Hindi. He spent a year studying at JNU, New Delhi before going on to University of Berkeley (California). He's acted in an award-winning Bhutanese movie, *Travellers and Magicians*. All this he tells me in a gentle, modest and self-effacing manner. Some more chat and Tshewang says he wants to interview me for his weekly TV show. Was that OK with me? 'We'll shoot outdoors with you sitting on your bike.'

He rushes out of the room again and returns with information that his camera and sound teams are setting up their equipment outside and we can go join them.

The idea was for me to ride into view and stop at a chalk-marked spot in front of the camera. Tshewang would ride pillion, get off and start asking me questions. It was all to be extempore.

Tshewang borrows a helmet for himself and we get a BBS car to take us to Centre Mall to collect the bike. In the car, we conduct a quick rehearsal. He asks about my journey, about what I think of Bhutan and my opinion on their upcoming first-ever general elections. In one answer I mention the Dalai Lama but Tshewang says I can talk freely about any and everything on earth except the Dalai Lama.

It is a short ride to my hotel. I go up to my room to get my own helmet. When I return to the hotel's parking lot, I find my new friend perched up on the seat, holding the locked handles, enjoying a simulated bike ride. 'I just love this bike,' he says and gets off.

With so much love heaped on it, the engine is happy to fire at the first kick and with Tshewang sitting pillion, I ride back to BBS, passing on the way a white Maruti van with its windows rolled up, shaking as if it has Parkinson's. I hear muted sounds of two males singing. My would-be taxi drivers were still at it!

As we pass the BBS gate, the cameras begin to roll. I come to a stop at the chalk mark and switch off the engine. Tshewang gets off and we both remove our helmets.

'Welcome to Bhutan,' Tshewang says to me in English and Hindi. Then the questions begin.

Why am I travelling on a motorcycle at my age?

How was the journey?

Did I have any problems?

What do I do in Pune?

What types of speech problems do I deal with?

What do I think of Bhutan's upcoming elections?

What is my opinion on the newly signed Indo-Bhutan friendship treaty?

For the hour it takes to shoot this 30-minute film, I feel like a movie star, a guru, an adventurer, a healer and a political analyst all in one!

Once the shoot is over, Tshewang says we must have lunch which, not having had breakfast, I think is a capital idea. BBS has an open air staff canteen set next to the landscaped front gardens. Tshewang and I join a group of ladies. I wonder why they are dressed to the hilt and why their perfectly made up faces seem familiar till Tshewang tells me two of them are newsreaders and the other three act in a serial. I've probably seen them on TV. They are all dressed in colourful *kiras*; their national costume. Coffee drunk, I take out my cigarette pack, expecting someone to say this was a No Smoking Zone. But the opposite happens. First Tshewang and then all the five ladies want a smoke too. The ladies take dainty puffs and blow smoke in each others' faces and laugh.

I like the unabashed manner in which everyone in Bhutan asks me for a cigarette. From the policemen at the Chuka check post to these glamorous TV stars, they all seem to enjoy smoking. Maybe because they rarely get the chance to smoke.

Sandwiches consumed and happy goodbyes said, the ladies go into the adjacent building, housing the studios while Tshewang Dendrup leads me back to his office. We've become friendly. He's enthusiastic about my offer to conduct a speech workshop for the newsreaders and says he has to discuss the idea with his boss. He goes out of his office saying he'll try and organize it for this very afternoon. I am left to wait for half an hour. He returns with the news that his boss has liked the idea, an interdepartmental memo has been sent and available staff members would attend the workshop scheduled for 3 pm. Is that okay with me? 'Sure,' I say, delighted that my morning's wish was actually coming true.

The sixteen women and men who attended were each rated for speech clarity, voice quality, rate of talking and power. Suggestions for improvement were well received and, for an impromptu workshop, it all went well enough for them to end it with a 'thank you party' in the garden canteen where I got another chance to feel like Santa when the ladies asked me for cigarettes. Tshewang handed me CDs of the unedited 'rushes' copy of our interview and his movie. I ride back to Centre Lodge half hoping to find the rollicking hash smokers and maybe breathe some more of their passive smoke. It certainly brought me good luck in the morning.

There are no white vans shaking with mirth anywhere

along the road back to the hotel. Back in my room, I exhibit no hesitation in reaching out for the now almost empty bottle of Old Monk. I have one last cigarette left but this is also my last night in Bhutan.

By tomorrow evening, I should be in Siliguri.

Back to India

MY LAST MORNING in Happy Country has begun with a flurry of activity. I've packed up, carted the bags down the narrow stairway, paid the happy lady on the first floor, arranged for a taxi (a WagonR) to Phuntsholing and got back to the GREF campus in Simtokha. The plan is to get the bike loaded on one of their trucks which bring in building materials from India every day and ply back empty. The bike will be offloaded at the New Jalpaiguri Railway Station (Freight Area) and put on a train to Pune via Kolkata. I'm also sending away the saddle bags packed with the biker paraphernalia I will no longer need. I'm looking forward to having just a backpack to carry. I'm booked to fly out of Bagdogra tomorrow.

Time begins to move faster than it has in this last languid week I have lived amongst the most unhurried people in the world. Today I am already in Simtokha and it is not 8 am yet.

The truck is waiting and all I have to do is ride up the 45 degree ramp and let the two soldiers in there take her. They secure the bike with ropes to metal rings on the side. Once the half door of the truck clangs shut and the truck departs I suddenly feel incomplete as if a part of me is gone.

The taxi driver has followed me and is waiting outside, at the gate. He is the tallest Bhutanese I've seen—6 feet 5 inches at the very least. Like all of his countrymen that I have met (except perhaps Pema Dorji, the woman hater in Gedu), this giant of a man has an air of gentle pleasantness about him. He slides into the driver's seat with his scalp brushing against the car's roof. As we get ready to leave I see an officer in uniform come out of the gate and approach the driver. 'Phuntsholing?' he asks, then spotting me comes over to my side of the car and greets me with a cheery 'Hi'. He is looking for a ride to Phuntsholing. Can he come with us?

Glad for company after days of talking with myself, I say, 'Yes, of course!'

By the time we pass the Chuka check post, I have learnt that Major Gaurav Rai is an instructor at the Army Aviation Corp and is currently posted at the Sewak Road Base in Siliguri where he trains pilots to fly the army's French Alouette helicopters. He flies regular sorties to the China border in Sikkim.

Engrossed in talk, exchanging views on everything from politics to Royal Enfields to flying ultra-lights, we are blind to the Bhutan rushing past us outside.

We stop at the GREF canteen, where I had met the American bikers last week, and this time there is space at the tables for us to sit and partake of the canteen's delicious fare. The Major tells me he has a jeep parked in Phuntsholing and plans to drive it to Siliguri today. I can come with him if I like. He can even arrange to put me up in the officer's mess where he himself stays. I've told him I have a plane to catch tomorrow afternoon. He says the Bagdogra airport is only 20 kilometres from his base and he can arrange for someone to drop me there.

We are now passing the TALA Campus, Gedu. I pull out my cell phone and dial Commander Phurpha's number. His loud jovial voice comes on line. He is talking from his village some distance from Gedu. In his broken Hindi he invites me to visit Bhutan again. He puts in a few words of praise for India. 'India Bhutan *bhai bhai*,' he says. Then, abruptly switching subjects he informs me that he has given up alcohol. *'Hum abhi nahi pita hai,'* (I don't drink now) he says, sounding only half convinced. I look at the clock on the dashboard which glows 14:30. I tell Phurpha I'll call him again in the evening to check if his resolution is still holding. The car turns a bend and the connection begins to break. I hear staccato bursts of Phurpha's loud guffaws before we are cut off.

Soon we are in Phuntsholing. The Major guides the taxi driver to the GREF parking lot where amidst trucks and buses stands an olive green jeep. An orderly waiting next to it salutes the Major and hands him the keys. He says the tank is full and a thermos of coffee is in the jeep as the sahab had ordered.

The Major seems to be in a hurry to leave. 'I have a training flight at 7 am tomorrow,' he explains hoisting himself into the driver's seat. I do the same on the passenger side and we are off.

The sun is setting as we come out of Bhutan gate where a long queue of departing Indian labourers has formed as they cross back to Jaigaon after a day's work. Beyond the gate everything is exactly as it was a week ago. In sharp contrast to the silent lonely streets of night time Thimpu, Jaigaon is pulsating with activity. It is noisy. It is crowded. The traffic is chaotic. Gaurav has driven on this road many times and deftly manoeuvres the jeep through the melee but it is slow going. Night has set in by the time we come to Dalgaon and get on to NH31C.

Gaurav and I have established a good rapport and are down to sharing views on women as married men are known to do when they are out of ear-shot. I'm expecting to hear some raunchy stories but I learn that the dashing pilot sitting next to me is going through divorce proceedings and that he has a five-year-old son. They had married eight years ago but had spent most of them living away from each other. She couldn't leave her job in Kolkata to join him where he was posted. Finally they had decided to part. The son would live with her. He was alone again. Then he begins to apologize for 'boring me' with his problems and tries to return to his previous jolly manner but the sombre mood in the jeep prevails right until we arrive at the Sewak Road Air.

My benefactor quickly gets me set in a suite of my own. From the balcony, I can see a wall of tall trees which Gaurav says is the southern boundary of the Chapramari Wildlife Sanctuary. 'That is an elephant path right there,' he points out into the darkness but it all looks black to me. Last week seventy-two elephants had passed by the balcony one behind the other. I mention my own encounter with the pachyderm and he says I was lucky. Elephants are dangerous. Only last month two young officers on a morning stroll had been killed by a bull elephant in heat. The animal had suddenly appeared out of the jungle and attacked them. There had been many other people around but no one could do anything except watch in horror as the men were being mauled. He says elephants regularly stray on to this campus. When they do, sirens are sounded and all the gates are thrown wide open allowing the beasts unhindered access to wherever they want to wander. Nothing can stop them. 'Everyone is to stay a minimum 300 feet away from them,' he tells me in soldier-speak.

Gaurav has to be on duty by 6 the next morning so we say our goodbyes and hope to meet again somewhere sometime. I watch him walking away in the long corridor that separates our rooms. Was it only 12 hours ago that we met?

I switch off the lights and lie on the bed. In less than a minute, news of my arrival must have gone viral in the mosquito-world because a couple of pioneers are already humming welcome songs in my ears. I get up and forage through my backpack for the bottle of repellent I hadn't needed all through my stay in Bhutan. No mossies in Bhutan. One more reason to be happy!

The night is alive with sounds of the jungle—a zillion crickets screeching away, owl hoots responding to each other, a rustle of breeze. And then… the non consciousness of sleep masks everything out.

Go Air's Bagdogra-New Delhi flight is cruising at 33,000 feet and I'm in the window seat looking at a carpet of white clouds, thinking about all the places underneath that are hidden from my view. The Airbus makes mockery of the days I spent riding the terrain below, by speeding over it in minutes. I can't see Kurkure from here. I wonder if he's slicing onions for yet another chicken curry in Sohela? The tribal chicken thief, the stuttering Inspector Saha, the white-robed Jain nuns, the unhappily-married trash seller—all living their lives under the white clouds.

'Ladies and gentlemen, we will be landing in Delhi in a few minutes. Passengers are requested…'

I've changed planes in Delhi and will be landing in Pune soon. My month-long road journey is approaching its final minutes. I'm happy to see it end. I'm homesick!

After many nights of sleeping in different rooms, my brain now craves the familiarity of my own house.

It is harvest time once I'm back home. I'm king again! Juhi has hugged me and said, 'Wow' at least ten times before we've even got out of the airport. Meena has cooked my favourite dinner (guess what?) and even Bingo is looking at me with more respect.

Guess it was a good idea going to Bhutan!

Epilogue

I WENT TO Bhutan looking for Happiness but guess where I found it? In my own pocket! It had been riding with me all along. Maybe Bhutan provided the right ambience for it to express itself more freely. Maybe being aware that one was happy was the way to be happy? After all what was happiness but an emotion, and if, like the monk in Paro, one could enter a happy state of mind at will, I would've succeeded in my quest for it in the land of the thunder dragon.

The Bhutanese are aware that they are a happy people. You can see it in their eyes. You can hear it in their speech. Compassion, laughter, empathy and gentleness pervade the air here. There is love and respect for their king. There is no strife between groups of any kind. They all seem to agree with each other and their king. There are no religion-oriented conflicts. Corruption doesn't exist. There is no security-phobia in either the government or the people, no video cameras monitoring everyone. The Police are friendly and helpful. Crime is rare. Smiling seems to be everyone's favourite activity.

On the roads in India one is always on guard against conmen and various other hazards, but in Bhutan there were no such challenges. I didn't need to be wary. I could leave the back-pack hanging from the handle of my unlocked bike as I walked the streets of Thimpu and Paro, assured that it would be there when I got back.

Bhutan makes it easy to be happy and I basked in this liberating ambience for ten days. Every day merged predictably, securely and happily into the next. Everyone seemed to be living happily ever after.

But I couldn't; didn't really want to. Perennial happiness was all good as a theoretical concept but maybe the dish of life needed to be peppered with a few problems and salted with a pinch of anxiety if it was to be tasty? Because after ten days in paradise I had begun to miss the country next door where anything could happen and often did...

Acknowledgements

I AM GRATEFUL to Maj. Gen (Retd.) M S Pillai for his help during my stay in Bhutan and to Suresh Bhapkar for all that he did for me in Akola, Nagpur and Nagzira. I thank my sister Nimmi Harisinghani, Surekha Chandrasekhar, Alex Reisenbichler, Dr Prafulla Wani and Dr Krishnakant Shukla for their help in polishing up the narration.

I thank Kanishka Gupta of Writer's Side, my literary agent, for his confidence in my writing, and Sanghamitra Biswas of Westland for her encouraging editorial help.

I also thank my wife Meena and daughter Juhi for their enthusiastic and steadfast support while I was on the road.